ENTREPRENEUR - DOESN'T YOUR BUSINESS DEPEND ON IT?

The Mental Shifts You Need to Know Before
Taking the Jump Into Business

BENJAMIN BONETTI

www.truthpsychologist.com

WHAT ACTION ARE YOU GOING TO TAKE TODAY THAT CHANGES YOUR LIFE?

CONTENTS

Foreword   9

Chapter One – How To Turn Your Time Into Money   17

Chapter Two – Why You Need To Say Goodbye   49

Chapter Three – Why Being Busy Isn't The Solution   67

Chapter Four – Letting Go Of Ego   79

Chapter Five – Looking For Mentors   91

Chapter Six – What Are You Really Worth?   101

Chapter Seven – Establishing The Next Venture   115

Chapter Eight – Duplication Is The Answer   125

Chapter Nine – Inner Productivity And Purpose   135

Chapter Ten – What Next?   149

A Lesson On Breath   160

4 Week Productivity Diary   165

ACKNOWLEDGEMENTS

Everyone who doubted me!

FOREWORD

- What This Is Not
- What Qualifies Me

Okay, welcome to this book and let's get started. Firstly, I think it's important to understand what this book is *not*. This book is not your business bible, I've produced one of those in the past, outlining recommendations on the topics of marketing, advertising, networking and all things connected to getting started as an entrepreneur; it is not a book that promises to give you all the answers to every question you could ever ask or a book that attempts to condense 30, 40, 50 years of business experience into one easy-read of less than 200 pages, and it will not provide you with any shortcuts to reaching business financial targets.

There are no promises, no guarantees, and no secret formulas, but within the pages of this book I share with you my journey and the issues I have encountered through my experience of setting up multiple businesses. In so doing, I share with you everything I have learned, my learnings and my understandings, in a very simple and honest way, and I will attempt to cover all the mindful aspects that are often overlooked or, worse yet, not covered at all, as they can be deemed unimportant or insignificant in the early stages of setting up a business.

By highlighting these aspects now, I'm hopeful that when they come about, you'll be armed with a better understanding. It may not be now, it may be six months, six years or even further down the line from now, but these aspects will arise and the questions raised in this book will be asked. However, with this said, not every aspect or question raised in the following pages will be relevant to you but I invite you to listen, absorb and accept the information being shared.

Listen to the unique connections it makes with you and understand that as humans, we are only the by-products of the knowledge and the known we give ourselves... and the more we know, the greater our ability to act.

By understanding and accepting this, we give ourselves the ability to remove and break down the barriers associated with a lack of known and, in so doing, we become aware of and open to opportunities to increase our known by seeking help, learning more, and understanding more than we currently do. In the bigger picture, the more we know, the more we increase the likelihood that we'll make better choices that best represent a life filled with fulfilment and happiness, rather than accepting the life we've inherited as truth, without conscious control or design.

You see, I was trapped in this unproductive cycle for many years believing that others were better than me on the basis that their business appeared to be more successful than mine. They had more staff, they had a bigger house, or they had a nicer fleet of vehicles, but then I started to get into the nuts and bolts of the business world and the more I learned and understood, the more I began to realise that things are not always as they seem and appearances can be deceptive. Not all businesses are as healthy as they may appear on the outside.

Fulfilment is so much more than stuff; it starts and ends with an emotional connection and the levels of truth you are willing to go to right now. Are YOU willing to be truthful now so that you may remove any restrictions in the future? Or are you going to assume that everything will be okay and there is little need to make mental shifts?
This choice can only ever be <u>yours</u> to make but you have nothing to lose and everything to gain through just listening to what is written and finishing the book.

But you don't have to take just my word for it...

"Benjamin didn't make sense at first. I walked out of the event confused over what was about to happen, but then 17 months later I was faced with an issue and knew exactly what to do – he'd imprinted something and it worked, FANTASTIC."

Cutting the BS

You may be wondering what qualifies me to write this book, part of the <u>truth series,</u> on business? Well, for starters, I run and own many successful businesses. I have bought and sold businesses and flipped them and I have built businesses from the ground up into some of the most internationally recognised within the self-help field.

I'm not a textbook-trained business owner, there are ample more qualified individuals in this field than me – you only need to look at local universities to find various business strategists with any amount of degrees and doctorates to understand what I mean by this – but I have, however, lived with the pain of having to lay off staff and friends when the market takes a turn for the worst.

I've been at the point where I've had to approach multiple banks for loans when my rent has been due; I've driven 100k vehicles straight out of the showroom and the following year traded them in for something 15 years older and valued at 5k; I've seen things from the gutter and I've seen things from the top, and all of this has provided not only value but also rooted my own beliefs based on a varying perspective.

So, what qualifies me to write this book? Nothing. No credentials, just an honest, real and truthful approach to business – mistakes (learnings) and all. Sure, I have plenty of paper qualifications but not one alone has provided the learnings I'm blessed with today. I am going to share with you everything I've learned, including the things I believe would-be business owners should understand before taking the leap into business.

I'm going to share with you some of the tools and techniques I use not only with my clients and 3-day Mastery Class participants, but also in other aspects of my businesses. As stated already, not everything I share with you in this book is going to make absolute sense right away or feel instantly relevant to your current situation, but I ask you to take on board what I'm teaching and accept my learnings so that in the future you may reflect on these points and use what you know to quickly understand and resolve the situations in question as they arise.

Let's get on with it; let's commit here and now. Let me help you on your journey. Use this book to generate further thinking and to address thoughts and ideas you've perhaps shelved in the past, and to relinquish all expectations.

Note: to use this book as intended, please fold over corners, write in the margins, circle words and underline text that you'd like to refer too in the future – this is your chance to map out the aspects of your mind that you've perhaps pushed in to the corners as insignificant.

I am not a puppet…

Life is an illusion.

You create your own yardstick.

THERE ARE NO SECRETS TO SUCCESS.

DOESN'T YOUR BUSINESS DEPEND ON IT?

CHAPTER ONE – HOW TO TURN YOUR TIME INTO MONEY

- Understanding the Emotional Connection
- The Shifts You Need to Make Before You Commit
- Why I've Never Looked Back
- Security Is a Myth

I was brought up in the 80s (very fortunately) with the understanding that anything is possible. My parents believed anything was possible and it was my understanding that I could be or have anything I wanted, and I could travel the world and connect with anyone I wanted. I had what could be considered an upper middle-class upbringing with good schooling, a father who worked long hours but was rewarded with all the expected norms (as projected by the media) in society at the time – new BMW every few years and Caribbean holidays – and things I only came to appreciate in adulthood and still reflect upon today.

I had everything I was supposed to have... until the day I was told that things wouldn't be the same for me; that society was moving and education would be the key to all successes and without it I'd be at risk of being unable to sustain the lifestyle I'd encountered as a child for myself and my own family. Looking back, along with these comments came a lot of restrictions, albeit unintentional. This was now an environment in which education was the primary focus; technology was working its way into the banking system and every other professional environment and it seemed that without a university degree, an introduction via my father or his connections just wouldn't cut it or guarantee my own successes as it had done for generations before.

It was at this point that I was introduced to the belief that education was the way; that education was the root to all successes and without it I'd be left on the side-line. This belief structure followed on through my primary school years and into secondary school, with many people believing that the traditional route of school, college and university was the only route to financial freedom, and the only route to success, fulfilment and the bigger and better things in life was to have a career within a professional environment. I subscribed to this belief of fulfilment in life being found through a solid education, a good job and high pay-cheques opening the doors to having more, and I subscribed not because I didn't have the intelligence to see things differently but because I didn't know any other way – and neither did anyone else in my social network.

At the time, I remember thinking that this life of fulfilment was perhaps out of my reach. I was academic, but the choice to spend fifteen or twenty years in education was not something that particularly excited me; I wasn't as passionate about becoming a doctor, a lawyer, or an accountant as some of my peers, and I couldn't see myself sitting behind a desk for 60 years, retiring, and then popping my clogs seven years later. There had to be more to life than this, surely – wouldn't it make more sense to work for seven years and then retire for 60 more?

You see, I wanted my life to be more fulfilling than that. I wanted my life to work in alignment with adventure, to leave a legacy, and I wanted to utilise my work and understanding as well, sharing my story to build an income. I wanted to build a lifestyle that would suit my needs in life, inspire others to do the same, and I wanted to build something that could support me 24hrs per day, 365 days per year, with limited overheads or staff, and could function while on vacation with no geographical restrictions.

"Impossible…" so I joined the Army.

During my time in the military, I came to understand that the perception of another and the belief of another is not necessarily truth, and what's believed true by one individual is not necessarily true to me or to you. It wasn't until I shifted into this new space, this new understanding, that I came to realise how so many attachments in life come down to the value associated with money. **You see, money gets a bad name.** There are so many different aspects to money, and there are so many motivating and driving forces to having money. But it's not money that dictates how much time you have available to spend with the family, how many nice things you have or anything else for that matter, it's the values you have placed on it.

Let me briefly explain what I mean by this. If it's your aspiration to spend more time with your family (one of the most commonly expressed regrets when people reach the end of life) and you believe to do so you need...

- a big house (5 bedrooms, 3 en-suites, double garage, large garden)
- nice cars (a family car and a saloon, all less than three years old)
- gym membership (which you use twice per week)
- stuff (new clothes every week and the latest 4K televisions)

... then you have mixed the values in terms of TRUE and PERCEIVED. You don't need any of the above to spend more time with loved ones, in fact, these things only restrict the amount of time you have when you take into consideration the amount of time required to finance them. Let's say your outgoings are $7000 per month and you're working a 40-hour week to make the payments; you could reduce your outgoings by living in a smaller house, driving less expensive cars, going for a walk instead of going to the gym, and buying less stuff. You could reduce your outgoings to $5000 per month, work less hours, have more time to spend with your loved ones and thereby achieve your aspiration.

In my world, money means simply one thing. Freedom.

The freedom to do as I please whenever I wish; for this, I truly believe that money is required, but I'm not talking about money in abundance. My monetary figure might be a lot less than the figure you believe is required to have the freedom you want, but it's a figure based on achieving the optimum amount of happiness and fulfilment in my life with the minimum amount of stress and pressure. If I have a roof over my head, food in the fridge, and enough left over to enjoy quality time with my children, then I can be comfortably assured that whatever it is I am doing is working. This may seem overly simplistic, I know, and it takes a whole new way of thinking to adopt this less can be more approach in terms of TRUE value, but when you chunk-down those connections, it always produces truth.

Of course, we are all different, and it's important to understand and realise that very often it's not the thing itself or the beauty of an object that we believe to be of importance or value, it's the emotional connection we've attached to it.

I find beauty in classic cars, much more so than in modern cars packed full of technology and gadgets. I find beauty in traditional coachwork engineering, in architecture and in aspects of past culture that offer certain emotional attachments and bring me happiness, yet within my businesses, I focus very much on the present and the future. I find beauty in the past because so much learning can be found there, but all of my focus and efforts are based on the emotional connection I have in the present moment and in that of future market needs.

So, if I asked you to list just three things that you want in life, right now, and then asked you to expand these things into the realms of emotional connections and attachments,

I'm fairly certain that whatever they are, they're going to be similar to those of your neighbour.

#1 What do you want in life?

_____

_____

_____

_____

_____

#2 What do you want in life?

_____

_____

_____

_____

_____

#3 What do you want in life?

_____

_____

_____

_____

_____

_____

From cars, houses, clothes, phones and even store labels, we perceive value and truth based on the values we have inherited – mostly without much (or any) conscious thought or consideration. We've been cultured to believe this is the truth, but I'm going to invite you to challenge these beliefs. I invite you to challenge whether this path offers what you really want, and question whether it offers true fulfilment. You don't have to adopt this approach forever, just until the end of the book.

Stop envying the life of others and design your own blueprint.

Before taking the plunge in any business venture or life changing choice, I always recommend chunking down to the specifics of the emotional connections. These may not necessarily be true emotional connections but rather perceived emotional connections, and this is because unless you have already experienced something as a direct result of this strategy (something we will cover later in the book) you can only ever be second guessing what the emotional connection would be.

If you are familiar with my online Truth Training programme, you may have heard me talking on the topic of perceived versus true values, and how you can have everything you want right now through visualisation. You see, despite what you might think, you don't need tangible items to be able to encounter and experience emotional connections. Visualising something can generate the same emotional connections as physically having that something, and the same dopamine releases can be triggered simply by closing your eyes and seeing, connecting and understanding what the vision you have of your future will bring when you have it.

CAVEAT: There is a big difference between having and visualising. Visualisation will not make items magically materialise, I simply recommend using this exercise to check-in with your thoughts on what you want and thereby make sure that whatever it is you're aiming towards and focusing on will actually bring about everything you think it will.

The invitation here is to think about the reasons *why* for a moment and to test-drive the reality you're aiming for. Spend just a few moments drafting out and understanding the connection you have with business, with money, and with having.

What does it all truly mean to you? Chunk it down to the specifics, to the point where you notice the emotional shift within; chunk down to the nuts and bolts of whatever this may bring.

The following questions may provide useful starting points and food for thought:

- Are you connected to money because it means you can show the people of your past that you are worthy?
- Does it come down to having time to share with loved ones; good quality positive time with loved ones?
- Does the enjoyment and purpose of money come down to their emotional connection and their memories, and how they will remember you?
- Does your connection to money come down to a past concern, a past restraint or a past belief of people you respected?
- Are you on a journey to prove all those who ever doubted you wrong?
- Are you on a journey to create a legacy based on inspiring future generations?
- Are you building a structure, an empire, to provide jobs; are you building something to provide brilliant memories for the people you care about?

It's important to take a moment to go through these prompting questions and understand the emotional connections you have, but if you're struggling, Tony's question to me may resonate with you right now…

Tony: *Benjamin, what does any of this have to do with my business, why don't you just tell me what to do to earn more and create more freedom?*

Benjamin: *Because **my** answers are based on **my***

direction, not yours!

You see, **your** reasons *why* are **your** key foundations, and the foundations of any business determine its success or failure. They determine the direction you go in and how stable the business becomes and remains in all aspects of progression. So, take just a moment now to draft out the emotional connections – what are the TRUE reasons why you are aspiring to achieve what you want?

TASK:

Chunk down to the nuts and bolts. The more specific you can be now, the more understanding you will have and the less you will need to reflect on and return to this key point. Go ahead, do it now; stop reading and start writing.

If you need to rest your mind further, I suggest reading through the meditation provided at the rear of the book.

_____

_____

_____

_____

_____

_____

_____

Okay, now that you have completed the task, you understand your own emotional connection with money and with starting your own adventure. The next step, and one that's of equal importance, is to understand the shifts you need to make to be able to shift your thinking!

The need for this shift is more common than you may think. Looking back, when I started my first business, I thought that because I had the textbook solutions to every business question, and the fact that I was able to confidently convince my bank manager to lend me more than 10 times my previous year's income, I was good to go.

But, I hadn't made the emotional shifts needed or understood the reasons why I was setting off on this journey – my own adventure. I am fully grateful for the bank loan that helped me to set up my first business, and I'm also grateful for the subsequent learnings that came my way through reckless spending, and the understanding I gained of the differences between successful businesses and those operating within a debt culture. Since those days, I have not borrowed another penny in any of my businesses and I reinvest continually to free up my time.

You see, as you develop and grow as a business owner, you will also develop and grow as an individual. Setting out without an understanding of the reasons why, or without an understanding of the emotional connections driving your actions may simply magnify the person you are now. Don't you deserve to be more than you are right now? Avoid the temptation to fear these shifts, or fear becoming more of the person you want to be.

Don't you deserve to be more than you are right now?

_____

_____

_____

_____

_____

_____

What shifts do you need to make in your own BE-ing?

_____

_____

_____

_____

_____

_____

It's nurturing the land and culturing yourself into a place of being that you are happy to magnify and project x10 that not only determines and inspires self, it gives you choice. You can choose to make the shifts needed to let go of some of those attachments and to shift into a new mindset and a new belief structure, releasing the negative connotations of the past, or you can choose to stay as you are – restricted.

Before you set off on your business journey and adventure, pause for a moment and think back to the shifts you should make before setting out. If you are already working within a business, then take a moment to think about the changes you could make right now that would release any restrictions.

_____

_____

_____

_____

_____

What is required now and why have you avoided taking this action in the past?

_____

_____

_____

_____

_____

_____

If you were to fast-forward 10 years from now, what advice would you be giving to the you of today (the previous version of self) before starting out?

_____

_____

_____

_____

_____

_____

It's important at this point to clarify that I'm not talking about learnings that come through being a business owner, an entrepreneur, or a human evolving and developing, I'm talking about the mental approaches you would have shifted.

Some will argue that if they knew what changes they

would have made and what advice they would be giving themselves 10 years from now, they would have made those changes and done it that way. Well, I'm not so sure that this is absolute truth. I think that as humans we all know what shifts we need to make; we all know where our weaknesses lie; we all know where further development is required, and we all know whether we can be healthier, happier, fitter, and with less stress, less anxiety, less anger and frustration in our lives. We know, but do we act? Even with all this knowing, if we fail to resolve and take action **right now**, we only magnify the picture and waste energy backtracking.

Think about it for a minute; what past issues have you not resolved which then manifested into something unnecessary; something that didn't need to be as big and as bad as it was? To remove this past strategy, what shifts do you need to make in your mindset and in your belief structure now, before you move forward?

What would happen if you failed to address these concerns or issues and continued as you are on your business venture?

_____

_____

_____

_____

_____

What if, due to business growth, there wasn't time to pause over the next three years. How would these issue be magnified and how would they restrict you from realising your true potential and the true scope of what is possible?

So, stop right here, and jot down the reasons why you should be making these shifts right now.

- What shifts, if any, could happen in the next few moments without the need for planning or preparation?
- What shifts could you make over the coming minutes, days and hours, and how might the future look just by making those changes?
- By addressing the issues; by stopping right now, pausing and thinking for a moment, what shifts could you be making – what could you be doing?
- What shifts do you need to make before you commit?

When you've worked through the above, you will know what mental, mindful, spiritual, and emotional changes need to be made. Next, I'm going to invite you to shift your current thinking pattern.

If it was impossible for you to make a mistake, what more would you do and why?

I've never found myself reflecting on the past and viewing anything as a negative. Sure, there are plenty of aspects to being an entrepreneur and a business owner that with hindsight I would have changed, and some of my businesses haven't been as successful as I thought they would, but that's part of the journey and part of the excitement of potentially living the life YOU want.

The sooner you begin to understand the benefits found in any failure, the better. It's from these experiences that more learnings can be made, and more is learned from failure than from following the easy route.

I have learned over the years that in taking control over 'self' and taking control over my own destiny, I free up so many aspects of life and remain open to opportunities that may once have been lost through losing the ability to choose.

It's well documented that I left school at sixteen and joined the military in the same year. I joined as a boy soldier and worked my way up, going through military college before leaving in my early 20s. One of the benefits of being in the military is learning very quickly that age is nothing but a number. The amount of pressure applied to you as an individual forges a completely different character and personality to those out with the military or those who do not experience the same extreme pressures in this type of environment.

Anyone reading this with a military background or coming from a highly-disciplined background will understand the distinction that's being made here. I look back on those years and despite not always being happy with the decision I made to join the forces, I can still appreciate the time, the pressure, and all the work that was given to me as an individual. I appreciate the commitment of my sergeants and the officers, and the commitment of those who have built an infrastructure that has lasted hundreds of years and continues to base its practices on momentum – a constant forward direction.

I now know that the time I spent in the forces provided the pinnacle turning point in my belief structure. It allowed me to remove the limiting belief of education being the sole reason behind an individual's success, and it began an understanding that success is the result of an individual's beliefs, efforts and choices. We each have the choice to remain tied to the boundaries and limitations placed on us by the external world; the limitations and beliefs inherited by loved ones, parents, or teachers, or to set ourselves free and go beyond those boundaries. The forces provided me with a turning point, and it's a point from which I've never looked back.

I control everything within my life, a life in which the only truth is the truth that I create.

I now freely accept that I am the only author of my destiny. Knowing that it's only me who can make the choices to change, I have control over what I choose to accept or choose to decline, irrespective of the restrictive beliefs of others over what's possible.

However, this mindset was not always well received or accepted. Let me explain...

Having left the forces, I believed that having worked within this environment, managing teams of highly qualified individuals, and having qualifications would mean I could easily walk into the civilian world and I'd be fighting off potential employers. I was educated, had life experience, a proven team player, hardworking, loyal, well-travelled, honest, the list goes on.

Well, several hundred job applications later, I learned that perhaps my newly founded education, military experience and exemplarily military conduct upon discharge meant nothing. In fact, in one interview the interviewer expressed his view that my motivation, passion and drive could be a threat to him and his job. My passion, determination and self-belief, it seemed, were so strong that employers were turning me away because they were fearful of how quickly I might progress within their company.

WHAAAAT? My passion to deliver was threatening?

I had to eat, I had to pay my rent, and I had a child on the way. This forced me into several different circumstances, and these circumstances would yet again change my path and help forge my identity and my belief structure –

character building circumstances indeed!

I'd gone from eating in quality restaurants to scrubbing dishes behind the kitchen door, and working in security while maintaining a 9 to 5 job. But, you see, it was these very struggles that forged me into someone with a real understanding of what is truly possible – and it's the reason why I am sharing this with you now.

The past and the beliefs of another do not forge you as an individual; the perception of others and their perception of you has no meaning other than the meanings you willingly accept. You do not have to be washing dishes to forge this understanding, you simple have to listen and digest. If you are aware of Maslow's Hierarchy of Needs, you will know that security is up there with food. But, in my world, security is nothing but a myth, and gone are the days when there was such a thing as job security.

For example, in days of old, working for the government meant a guaranteed pension, and sadly many people in this day and age (especially in western culture) still grasp onto this post-war concept. Redundancy levels are higher than ever before, more and more businesses are outsourcing internationally to save on salaries, pensions are failing, and technology is taking over many key roles in the workplace, so security is no longer something to hold onto unless....

WE CREATE IT OURSELVES.

As food for thought, consider the following...

Recent studies carried out by academics at Oxford University concluded that around 50% of jobs in the US are likely to become automated through technological advances in the not-so-distant future. The bottom line is that job security is a thing of the past.

It was while I was up to my elbows in soapy water washing dishes in a restaurant kitchen that I made a vow to myself to never allow anyone to tell me what I could and couldn't do. I was going to create my own security and I was going to create my own destiny based on the standards I had set for myself. I was not going to accept any restrictions placed on me by the pressures of society and I was not going to fall into the trap of believing that the house I lived in, the car I drove or the amount of money I had in my bank account could determine the individual that I was. The façade that many of us place on show to the outside world means little in terms of true fulfilment and truth itself.

Think for a moment about the number of characters you play in an effort to lie to the outside world and create a perception of true freedom – does your social media profile represent the truth, or is it designed to fit in with what society tells us we should have in life? Does it show the reality, the truth; does it show the struggles and the pain experienced daily? The reasons behind this and the need to express it are topics for another day and beyond the scope of this book, but for now, and before moving on to the next chapter, I invite you to do a few things.

First and foremost, I invite you to be truthful with yourself and to understand why now is the right time for you to take action, and, crucially, avoid lying to yourself about the reasons why. Why is now the right time to regain control of your life, and why is now the time to stop following the crowd and stop doing what you're doing simply because it's what the masses are doing? Now is the time to stop and to take a moment to understand why you've been accepting of social pressures in the past; why you have attached certain meanings to tangible assets, and why you are now deserving of being aligned to the person you want to be. Now is the time to utilise your own strengths and inner understanding and see the benefits this will bring in terms of business growth and development.

PAUSE AND THINK!

Time Is Your Only Asset

Okay, so you've cleared out some of the baggage and you've created a better understanding of self as you move on into the next phase. It's now important to understand that time is the only real asset you have. From the minute you wake up in the morning till the time you go to sleep at night, the only thing you have in connection with and in perfect harmony with your client or your competitor is the value you have placed on time, and how it has been a conscious consideration when calculating your personal and financial worth. Time is not something that can be expanded, you cannot add an additional 24 hours to each day. Sure, you can work longer and harder but I'm not sure that that's the solution either. So, what I am going to invite you to do right now, today, is to change your belief about what is possible within your working day, and, as you progress through the book, I'm going to invite you to work less and work differently. Don't worry, I will show you how, and I will share with you the tools and techniques that have allowed me to grow my business internationally and allowed me to produce several best-selling books that have been sold to over 1.8 million people globally.

You see, the only thing that we can utilise in every sense is time. Your minute and my minute mean exactly the same thing. The only thing that differentiates us as humans, apart from the emotional connection and the knowledge and understanding we have retained and regurgitated as knowledge, is time. Your minute and my minute are identical. The minute I have is identical to the minute the people I aspire to be have. So, how do you turn your time into money? I asked this question at the opening of a seminar I delivered last year: how do you turn your time into money? Well, it's very simple. Utilise it in a way in which there is a market need. Utilise it in a way in which that minute has a financial value, in a way that truly works with you as opposed to in a way that's perceived to be true by the rest of the market.

You see, if I priced my minute at ten thousand dollars and you priced yours at one dollar, over the space of a year and minute by minute my wealth will be greater. Turning your wealth around and turning your business into something that you are proud to call your own comes down to the value that you have placed on your minute.

- Now, if I was to say to you that you have ten minutes a day to work and you have a figure in mind that you need to clear every day, then what would that minute be worth to you?
- How many dollars per hour or how many dollars

per minute would you need to have or come up with for your current lifestyle to be moved onto the next level?

- How much money per minute would be enough for you to sustain your current level of growth and development?
- And how much per minute do you need to earn to live the in the way you do currently?

Once you have established the above, you can begin to reverse engineer how you are spending your time. If your goal and aspiration is to have an increased element of freedom and you know that you need to clear a thousand dollars a day, then you need to understand the monetary value of each and every one of your minutes and you need to make sure that you are being as productive as you can be within the time you have. If you then need to clear two thousand dollars a day, you need to increase the value you place on each minute.

You see, the amount of energy you disperse in each minute is identical, no matter what the amount of money you place on it, and the amount of money held within any minute could vary depending on how much you value that minute. Looking at it this way and placing values on minutes may seem slightly daft, but when you're wasting a minute or when you're procrastinating over a minute, you're also wasting and delaying the inevitable. Time is money and money is time. Have you begun to undervalue your time? Have you been freely giving away your time, and have you been utilising your time in the most effective way, the way that is going to support you as an individual?

Consider this: how much time do you invest in personal growth and development each day, and how much time do you invest in menial tasks that fail to support you and the person you want to become each day?

The more you utilise time as your key influencer to success, fulfilment, and to growth and development, the more you will radically start to change your perception of the outside world. For me, gaining an understanding of how I was spending my time allowed me to create strategic ways to reverse engineer my day so that I'd achieve X, Y and Z, and allowed me to look for the opportunities out there to support that.

As you may have heard me say in the past, we become the things we look out for the most. We become the things we focus on, so the more you shift into a space of appreciating your time, the more you understand what needs to be done and the less waste will occur. Money is your biggest asset, money is the key to freedom.

Most people remind themselves of the things they don't want and focus on that, they think of all the things that can go wrong and therefore attract those things into their life as a result of taking action on this – effectively working towards it. The shift here takes conscious effort.

Success, whatever that means to you, is brought about as a result of how you invest your time. **Time is your key to success.** Decide now what you are worth, how many minutes per day you are prepared to invest in self, what you need to earn per minute per day, and what needs to be done to maximise this potential; this earning.

Ask yourself where you need to go and what you need to do. The invitation here and now is to digest this, reflect upon it, and understand that you are only a by-product of the present moment. You are only a by-product of the minutes in each day and how they are spent and, as you know, ten minutes spent scrolling through social media can never be regained – it's lost time. Lost time equals lost opportunities, so whether it's lost to social media or watching your favourite soap on TV, unless rest and relaxation is the goal for those minutes, it's lost time that can't be recouped.

Remember, it's not about working more, it's about investing your time wisely. The more you start to add value and understanding to each minute, the more each minute means in terms of your future freedom, and the more you begin to make better choices over how your time is spent.

TASK:

The choice is yours...

What are you worth and why?

_____

_____

_____

_____

_____

_____

_____

_____

_____

_____

_____

What needs to be removed in your life in order to achieve this?

_____

_____

_____

_____

_____

_____

_____

_____

Why is now the right time to make the shifts happen for you?

_____

_____

_____

_____

_____

_____

_____

_____

_____

_____

_____

_____

_____

GREAT THINGS IN BUSINESS ARE NEVER DONE BY ONE PERSON.

DOESN'T YOUR BUSINESS DEPEND ON IT?

CHAPTER TWO – WHY YOU NEED TO SAY GOODBYE

- The New vs. Old Choices
- Why You Need New Friends
- Where to Go to Find Quality Connections
- Being Honest with You
- My Mistakes and Those Who Didn't Believe

Like all evolutionary journeys, there comes a point when you need to move into a new space; a point where the old version of you would have attracted certain things and the new version of you has attracted a completely different dynamic and a complete alteration in terms of what you previously felt was within the realms of possibility for you or even what you felt comfortable with.

If you have ever made a shift in your diet or your level of fitness, you will know exactly what I mean by this. The fatty, unhealthy, artificially coloured foods you once ate no longer seem appealing compared to the vibrant colours and tastes of the fresh fruits and vegetables you have switched to. A complete alteration takes place, and the same can be said when you make a shift in terms of the company you keep and the people you mix with, or the environment you immerse yourself in.

Important note: Sometimes a shift in the known produces a fear state of unknown. This fear, this unknowing, is a normal reaction and something *not* to fear – think about it.

You see, this was one of the biggest things I encountered when I set out on my own adventures as an entrepreneur, and one of the biggest frustrations I faced as a business owner and a human. I could not understand why others did not have the same passion and drive as I did, and I couldn't understand why so many people were comfortable in that space of being told what to do, then making mind-numbing career choices.

I could see no reason why others wouldn't find the same excitement in the changes that come with everyday life as a business owner and as an adventurer, but I remember one friend telling me that I should stop being so passionate. In fact, he said I shouldn't have the amount of inspiration and drive I had to achieve what I wanted in life because it was reflecting badly on him and others.

The people I thought were my friends, the people I thought had my back, were actually trying to pull me back into their space of comfort, holding me back in a space of acceptance for them – the reality they had created and the reality they wanted me to fit into. I truly believe they had the best intentions by saying what they did but, as I mentioned earlier, I'd already decided when I was up to my elbows in soapy water that nobody was going to tell me what I could or couldn't do.

The last thing I wanted to do, irrespective of the opinions of others, was to hold back. I didn't want to reach retirement only to look back with fear, frustration, envy and resentment. I vowed to myself that in every minute of every day I was going to do the best I could to inspire not only myself but others around me; to live with a smile and without a frown.

So, trust me when I say that you are going to be faced with some choices you will need to make, if you haven't faced them already. You are going to have conversations with people who will ask you why you are doing what you are doing, and they'll ask you in a negative manner. They ask not because they care, but because they can see the distance between you and them growing. They ask not because they are interested or inspired by you, but because you are threatening their own strategies and beliefs, and their own values about what is possible.

The invitation I extend to you here is to peel yourself away from these individuals. You can enjoy what was but understand that you are moving into a new space; you are creating a new version of the world for you and this is okay. It's exciting, and this shift will always offer a better alignment with what's truly important.

As an example, if one party in a relationship begins to take more of an interest in improving their diet and increasing their fitness levels, they shift into a new realm in terms of their eating and exercise habits. It's a common obstacle that this shift will then create a divide in the relationship with the distance between the parties growing. The positive drive and passion to make the shift and become healthier and happier effectively begins to create a barrier.

Are You Keeping Good Company?

The invitation here is to look at the person you want to become and to see if you are keeping good company; see if the individuals around you are supporting the future version of you, the person you want to become, and if not, consider if this reflects badly on them rather than you.

Consider also if these people fit into your new mould; can you see them in the new version of the world you're creating for yourself? As you do so, understand that it's okay to progress and it's okay to distance yourself from friends and people you once believed to be key elements of your life. Understand that I'm not suggesting you should cull your list of friends, I'm simply asking you to become more aware of the influences you are openly inviting into your space.

When I left to join the forces, I was away for differing lengths of time but I soon realised that every time I returned home and asked my friends what they'd been doing, I would get the same answers because they were still doing the same things. This was a pattern that was also noted by friends who travelled. They'd return from trips away with experiences and memories to share of new places and different cultures, but others in their social circles had nothing new to add to the conversation because there was nothing different or new going on in their lives.

Caveat: There is no right and wrong, there's just choice. If someone is happy living in that space then respect it! They will not respect your opinions unless they are the ones asking the questions. There is no truth apart from the truth you create; there is no author apart from yourself.

There is no truth apart from the truth you create.

As a business owner and entrepreneur, there are choices you are going to have to make soon about your future. There are certain things you are going to have to let go and the likelihood is that you already know what they are.

So ask yourself these questions...

- When will be the right time for you to make those changes?
- What needs to happen for you to speed up the process to deal with the inevitable before it happens?
- How long are you prepared to suppress your own dreams and legacy because of the fear of unproductive loss?

For me, the word **relationship** means simply to communicate; a communication vessel. Relate and Ship.

Who are you not communicating effectively with at the moment?

_____

_____

_____

_____

_____

_____

Where are there disruptions, and why are those disruptions there?

_____

_____

_____

_____

_____

You see, the frustrations of another often stem from their beliefs and values being challenged. You don't own that, you can't take responsibility for that, and only they have the choice of whether to accept or decline. We all have choice.

Right now, I'd like you to design and create a business identity for yourself. Begin by considering the following…

- What does that look like?
- What do you sound like?
- What do you feel?

Do you wake each morning feeling vibrant, happy and excited about going out to deliver and maximise your opportunities, or do you wake up and find yourself dealing with a barricade of comments and social media negativity and restrictions before you've even started your working day?

There is the old you and then there is the new you. The choices you have right now, today, depend on it, so what changes do you have to make and why?

_____

_____

_____

_____

_____

_____

Okay, with all of this said, I am going to invite you to make some new friends, meet new people, and socialise in environments that are going to support the new version of self. In the past, especially in an independent business I owned, it was key for me to network within the community of other business owners, not only to look for referrals but to build the image of my business and build an understanding of the needs and wants of my consumer in the process. I needed to meet new friends, and I needed to meet people who were going to support me on my journey; I needed to find quality connections.

The recommendation I want to make here is to understand the weaknesses you have and to find people who can support you, and vice versa. If you're not good with money management then find someone who can help you with that; if you lack creative ability then find someone who can help you to develop it (or do it for you), and so on.

Avoid the temptation to stay where you are because it's comfortable, and avoid the temptation to hold onto relationships that have been forged over time because you believe they mean something. You need to be honest with yourself; you need to understand that you are the by-product of the choices you make, and the choices you are making right now are either going to hold you where you are or they're going to move you on to the next level.

Now is the time to up your game.

Now is the time to better your game. Now is the time to reach out and forge new relationships with people who are more in alignment with the person you want to become. It's often said that you become like those you mix with the most, so in adopting this approach, you are surrounding yourself with people who represent your future vision of self. Are the people around you inspiring you to be bigger, greater, healthier, wealthier, happier and more fulfilled? Are they going to enable you to springboard onto the next level, or are they restricting you, keeping you boxed in, and fearful of your growth and development?

You Are Not Alone

There are ample online business forums and local community business support groups, and there are international networks that reach into the far corners of almost every nation. A quick internet search for "business networking in my area" will undoubtedly throw up a huge number of opportunities right on your doorstep, or you could go onto popular social media sites and search for business support or business networking and be amazed by the results.

Something I always say to emerging entrepreneurs and new business owners is to appreciate that everyone must start somewhere and we've all been there. Some established business owners appear to forget the apprehension or the way it felt to take those first steps into a networking meeting or even post those first few comments on social media forums, but we've all been there. You are not alone and the more you reach out and get involved in a growing network, the more you grow in terms of your business and personal development.

Now is the time to be totally honest with yourself.

Now is the time to be totally honest with yourself over who you are, what you want, and the environment you are currently in. Are you giving yourself the support you need, and are you supporting yourself in the most productive way? Are you mixing with people who are going to drive and inspire you to become more of the person you want to be, or are you putting yourself in environments that sabotage the potential of self? Are you seeking the best possible advice?

Where do you go when you need help?

_____

_____

_____

_____

_____

_____

I remember when I first set up my real estate business. Having worked in this line of business, I thought I had all the answers, but I soon discovered that having my own name above the door completely changed the dynamics of the business and my role. However, you can only ever sink or float and for me, floating was the only choice – my livelihood and my future depended on it.

So, without heeding the judgment and opinions of others, and without taking on the negative connotations society insists on placing on asking for help, I chose to be myself and get out there to find the help I needed: I networked. I was honest about what I needed from those around me and honest about letting those who could no longer support me in this realm play a lesser role in my life. Certain conditions were added to relationships, the first being that I needed to remove all of the drama from life. I needed to ensure that I was maximising every opportunity, and that every minute had value and purpose. If a relationship failed to fill a certain contract or criteria I had set for myself, then I would move on.

Entrepreneurs always drive on empty.

Avoid the temptation to fear judgment, it serves little value in business or in life. The title of my first book was *Entrepreneurs Always Drive On Empty* and it was chosen because it represented my early business networking days; days when my car's fuel tank was either empty as a result of networking, or empty because I didn't have enough money to pay for fuel to put in the tank. In those days, I had to wake at five in the morning to get to meetings on the other side of the county by 7am, and then very often I wouldn't get home until 10pm.

I now know that working such hours is not necessary; I have learned and developed since then, my knowledge and knowns have increased, but at the time, I got in my car and went out there. I knew who I needed to meet and I knew the types of people who'd be able to help me on my journey, my path to fulfilment, and it just so happens that those who were not supportive of me made the choice to remove themselves from my life.

These individuals were honest about their role in my destiny, my desires, and my legacy, making the choice to see a different path and go their own way, but this is not always the case, and this is when **the choice to move on becomes yours.**

The first choice you need to make is choosing who you want to become; not who someone else wants you to become or who society says you should want to become. Then, you must decide whether those around you are supportive of this choice. Are you keeping the best company? Decide what you need from others and, if this is lacking, where you can go to find it. What resources do you have available to you and what resources do you need?

Take an honest look at where you are investing your time and efforts in friendships, and question whether now is the right time to be investing in this field or whether a slight shift in the company you keep could move you into a space of greater growth, development and fulfilment. It's hard to return home to unsupportive relationships or to a partner who doesn't believe, and it's for this reason that your network, your support structure, and your infrastructure in business is supportive of the foundations you have set for yourself, and in alignment with your belief structure.

It's important to make these choices in the present moment and *not* to bury your head in the sand in the hope that things will improve and get better. Through making these choices you are designing and creating the life you want by surrounding yourself with people who can give you what you need, and in return you can provide them with what they need.

TASK:

What conditions are you going to apply to relationships from this point forwards?

_____

_____

_____

_____

_____

_____

What relationships do you need to move on from?

_____

_____

_____

_____

What relationships do you need to let go of?

_____

_____

_____

Who needs to let go of you?

_____

_____

_____

_____

_____

_____

I wasted plenty of time reinvesting in people who weren't prepared to listen and weren't on the same path or the same journey as me, so I can say with certainty that you need to avoid doing the same because you are simply delaying the inevitable.

IN THE BUSINESS WORLD, THE REARVIEW MIRROR IS ALWAYS CLEARER THAN THE WINDSHIELD.

DOESN'T YOUR BUSINESS DEPEND ON IT?

CHAPTER THREE – WHY BEING BUSY ISN'T THE SOLUTION

- The Difference Between Busy and Stupid
- Remove Yourself Two Days a Week
- Work Two Days a Week Flat Out
- Pricing Points: Charge More Work Less

Welcome to Chapter Three. In this chapter, I want to talk about why being busy is not the solution. In my coaching practice, and particularly in one-to-one coaching, people often tell me that they don't have time for X, Y and Z. As they see it, they don't have time to take themselves out of the business, and they don't have time to work on their personal development. They don't have time for whatever you care to mention, but the truth of the matter is **they need to *make* the time.**

This is something we spoke about in Chapter One. You need to make time, and you need to ensure that whatever it is you are doing is working towards the end result you want. You need to make sure you are utilising your time in the best way possible, and it all comes down to value; how do you value your time? What does every minute mean to you in a financial tone? What, financially, does one hour or 60 minutes-worth of work mean to you, and what does focusing 100 per cent without distraction mean to you?

Let's look at it this way; in monitory terms, how many hours or minutes do you need to work to achieve your aspiration or your goal for each day, week, month or year? You see, I know a lot of busy people, but I know a lot of poor people. By poor, I mean financially in this context, as opposed to spiritually, emotionally or any other way. So, to contextualise this, I know a lot of people who are very busy doing a lot of stuff that does not yield the results they want. They're busy, but what are they doing? I also know people who will procrastinate over a project for weeks on end and then eventually decide to employ someone else to get the work done. Being busy is different to being productive, and it all comes back to value, doesn't it?

What Are You Good At?

What if I was to invite you to do only the things you're good at; to be a professional only in the one specific thing you're good at and outsource or employ other people to do the rest – how much more productive would you be? If you could wake up in the morning, dedicate five hours to work doing only what you're good at and hand the rest over to others, whether it's designing, marketing, networking, sales or otherwise, how much more productive could you be?

This is a very interesting concept and one that's almost common sense, yet it's frequently neglected, especially by start-up entrepreneurs who think they can be all things to all people and that they have the tool for every task. But, let's delve a little deeper into things. If you can earn $100 an hour designing a flyer, is making the sales call the most valuable and productive use of your time? If you can hire a graphic designer for $30 an hour and you're earning $100 an hour, then wouldn't it make sense to employ an expert within that field to take care of these aspects for you?

As another example, if a marketing consultant is going to cost you $700 a month but from that yield you earn $7000 a month in client sales, would it not make sense for you to employ a professional in that field? If bookkeeping is going to take up a whole day each month and each day equates to $100 in lost earnings, would it not make sense to employ a professional in that field?

You see, in order to grow and develop, you need to be excited, and to be excited, you need to be doing only what you want to do. It's as simple as that. There are no hidden secrets, there are no hidden answers, that's it. Take my coaching practice as an example: I am a creator, I enjoy resolving issues, but I enjoy working with people I want to work with and I *only* work with people I want to work with.

Why? Because through pre-vetting people in an initial interview, I can assess how ready they are to listen and how much they believe I can make a difference. When they're ready, I know that when I'm speaking to them, I'm immersed 100 per cent in the present moment, my mind is not elsewhere.

I'm a great believer that we each have a unique skill set, a set of skills that are individual to us and no one else on the planet can deliver them. I might know that I have an eye for detail, but I also know that I don't have the knowledge to create flyers. I know what I want, but I don't have the technical skill to produce it, so why would I waste my time and effort doing something I wasn't skilled at or an expert in?

This is where I believe many starting-out entrepreneurs fail, and many others along the way. They immerse themselves in the things they're not skilled enough to deliver, resulting in the creation of content, products or services that aren't as good as that produced by those who are streamlined. They need to evaluate and understand their skills and, most importantly, they need to be honest with themselves so that what they deliver is truly their expertise.

There is a big difference between busy and stupid and smart and busy.

There is a big difference between busy and stupid and smart and busy. To be smart and busy (or not so busy), I reverse engineer my years, months, weeks, days and hours in advance. This allows me to focus only on the present, knowing that I've already created a strategy for the weeks and months ahead, and I've allowed enough contingence to be able to work two days a week with clients and three days a week working on new projects and the stuff that excites me; the stuff that gives me more freedom and more choice. One day each week is spent learning and developing my knowledge and my understanding of the world around me and beyond. It doesn't matter in what context, it might be architecture, art, history, geography, religion, science, we all could be more. But, to *be* more, we need to let go of certain things. We need to ensure that we're utilising our time in the most productive way and that we're getting the most out of every waking minute. To do so, we need to offload the things we're not good at.

How much more productive would you be if you only had to focus on doing the things you wanted to do?

Social media appears to be the big driving force in today's world (if social media is to be believed) with many social media experts offering their services, guidance and advice. But, the truth is, we could all manage our own media account, or we could outsource it to someone with the skills to manage it for us. If your key focus is to increase the number of clients you have and you outsource your social media to experts who know exactly how to go about it and present potential clients with exactly what they want and, in the meantime, you're getting on with fulfilling your role in the business, the role you enjoy, what would your turnover look like? What would your cost per hour look like?

An increase in the number of clients and the increase in demand for products or services brings with it the opportunity to increase volume or increase price, and increase sales opportunities. So, if you were to take up the invitation to work flat-out for just two days each week and utilise the remaining three days to expand, develop and grow your business, what would the next year look like? Whether developing and growing meant time spent strategizing or learning, what would it look like and what would it mean for you over the next 12 months? I learned a long time ago that as I developed as an individual and thereby created more value in myself and my skill set, the more I became able to increase my fees and work less while still maintaining the lifestyle I wanted. I built my cost per minute. You see, the choices are right there; you have the choice to continue along the path of being busy but ultimately unproductive, or you have the choice to do what you're good at – **be smart and become *less* busy.**

Become an Expert

In my world, busy is not sensible. Learn more and expand more in your field. Become an expert in your industry. Take a moment now to think about your year ahead, and then work backwards, incorporating all the time you need to grow and develop as an individual *and* grow and develop as a business. Consider the time you need to think, create, expand, and work both within and on the business.

As a recommendation to my clients, I advise scheduling just five things into each day: two large things and three smaller things. We all know that some days simply don't go to plan and stuff comes up, conversations take longer than anticipated, hold ups occur with suppliers or distributors, and a whole array of other unforeseen delays can creep into your day, and then something that should have taken minutes suddenly ends up taking hours. Stuff happens, and if you've got more than five things scheduled for the day, these delays make it quite unlikely that you'll achieve them all. However, with a limit of five things, you are much more likely to achieve your targets for the day, every day –

you're making the most of every minute you have.

I invite you now to explore this concept. Explore what you could outsource and what would allow you the freedom to focus on your skill; what would give you the freedom to focus on what you're good at? What would give you the freedom to do as you pleased, the freedom to remain excited and passionate and, most importantly, passionate about what you want to do and who you want to become?

Sadly, in my 14 years of coaching industry experience, I've met hundreds, if not thousands, of business owners who have lost sight of their original intention. In most cases, the original intention behind setting themselves up in business was either to have more time with their families or create greater financial wealth, but they completely lose sight of this. They lose sight of what it was they wanted, and they lose their identity as they become immersed in the business. To avoid this, you need to know what you want, and you need to remove the busyness of business.

The Busyness of Business

Removing the busyness comes down to focusing on being in the present moment, knowing what you want to do, and avoiding the temptation to overload – or create more to do just for the sake of appearing busy. Avoid slipping into the mindset that by doing more you're saving more, because this is rarely the case. The financial cost of outsourcing can make it a daunting prospect, but this is easily overcome when you consider the true cost of *not* outsourcing. If an expert can complete your project or your requirements in a tenth of the time it would take you, then you have created a huge saving in time and it's time that you can spend doing what you do best, thereby maximising the value of every minute.

Stop here for a moment before moving on. Think about your business and the areas of your business that are consuming the biggest proportion of your time. Consider how perhaps only a slight alteration, a slight shift in your mindset, could potentially produce more time in which to be doing what is most productive, not only for you in terms of your aspirations and the meanings you've attached (Chapter One) but also in terms of your bottom line. Could you increase your budget, your income, and your net worth?

EFFORT ONLY FULLY RELEASES ITS REWARD AFTER A PERSON REFUSES TO QUIT.

DOESN'T YOUR BUSINESS DEPEND ON IT?

CHAPTER FOUR – LETTING GO OF EGO

- Why I Didn't Buy the Car – Invest
- The Planets Won't Ever Align
- Turn Up and Expect More
- Outsource to Speed Up
- Know What You Need to Earn

Ego is a funny thing: it's an emotion, a connection to something in which we've created a meaning that represents little or no truth to anyone apart from self. It's a behaviour, and one we demonstrate through fear, although many would perceive it to be truth.

I remember a time when I had become so fixated on a car, and the meanings I had attached to the ownership of such a car, that when I finally achieved it and I was driving it for myself, I became terribly disappointed. I believed that driving this car and owning such a car meant something, that it had purpose and value, but in the development of self over the last ten years, I have stripped back the meanings attached to materialistic aspects of life and begun focusing on truth, the true meanings attached to being an entrepreneur and being an inspiration, and the connection I have by sharing my story. Since that moment, when owning the car proved to be a negative experience, producing an unproductive state, I've made some key choices and made some key shifts in my own thinking, including the value of self and where my time can best be spent as discussed in the last chapter.

Being, Not Having

In this chapter, I'm going to invite you to shift your thinking and remove any ego states. This means removing the state of cause and effect, and of having ownership, and relinquishing any ideas you have created for yourself over what ownership will bring in the future. But, this is going to be a difficult mindset-shift for entrepreneurs and business owners who have set out to achieve based on having as opposed to being. If this is you, your goals in setting up your business will have revolved around ownership of X value of property, X value of watch, X value of car, a diamond ring, and a list of materialistic possessions.

With this being the case, I would urge you to go back to Chapter One and reconsider. Now is the time to shift into a mindset of finding true fulfilment in non-materialistic aspects of life and in so doing, create a legacy for you based on being free as opposed to having. It's my belief that being true to self, being in alignment to the person you want to become, offers all those havings, they are simply the by-product of the being.

Focus on the being as opposed to the having.

Being. The more you focus on being the person you want to be, the more your business will grow and give you the financial freedom you deserve and desire to have. With this financial freedom comes the ability to have, but if the key focus is on the having as oppose to the being, you may find that in times of financial debt, unwanted emotions and behaviours will increase. Through owning the car I believed I wanted, I learned a valuable lesson. I sold it. I had to let go of ego, leave the ego-state at home, leave it out of the equation completely and invest the finance in growth and development.

Now, I know plenty of people who would rather spend $1500 per month on car repayments than personal growth and development but, for me, the only investment in a car that should be made is when the car becomes an asset, whether it's tax deductible, efficient, serves a value in which it gives a return, or is an investment based on future worth. I appreciate that this is quite an odd way of thinking, especially for those of you reading this book who invest heavily in car repayments (a depreciating asset) but all I am asking you to do is invite the part of the brain, the part of self that knows and understands what I mean here, to perhaps shift in thinking and avoid the temptation to lie to self and truth.

This shift relates to not only the car but other aspects of life; this shift involves removing the lifestyle that serviced all the aspects of living in a debt state and everything living in a debt society brings. It means removing the ego from the equation and starting to invest in aspects of self that matter. Invest in the business. Invest in aspects that will produce growth and development, aspects that will bring greater financial reward, greater security, and create the potential to have a positive impact on the lives of more people through the services you provide.

TASK:

What are you paying out right now that is not an investment?

_____

_____

_____

_____

_____

What are you paying out right now that is not being utilised to its true financial value?

_____

_____

_____

Where can you start to make some changes?

———————————————————————

———————————————————————

———————————————————————

———————————————————————

———————————————————————

———————————————————————

Okay, you've now revisited and realigned the financial aspects of where you are investing, reinvesting or spending. You've also created a mindset of utilising your time in the best and most productive way, giving you the best possible return. Now it's time to start looking at opportunities. It's time to look at when to take the step forward, when to take action and implement the aspects of your business that you have been delaying or procrastinating over for a long time.

The truth is, **there will never be a right time**: the planets will never align, ducks will not file into a neat row, and there will always be another reason for failing to take any action. But, if you start today, tomorrow will be easier. This is a concept that most of us are familiar with yet it's a concept that many business owners and individuals fail to understand and implement. By doing something today, no matter how small, it will get the ball rolling and begin creating the opportunities of tomorrow. There will never be a right time and we only have the present moment to operate in. Markets will always fluctuate; the dollar, pound and yen will never be stronger than one another without another market being higher or lower, and interest rates will never be as low as they were or as high as they are. The choice you have now is to start; the choice you have now is to invest, and the choice now is to make sure that tomorrow can be greater and more successful than today.

What actions are you *not* taking right now?

_____

_____

_____

_____

_____

_____

Why are you fearful of those actions?

_____

_____

_____

_____

_____

What happens if you fail to take the action needed tomorrow?

_____

_____

_____

_____

_____

_____

We can all procrastinate – I've been there. I've put off speaking to the bank manager and avoided conversations that should have taken place much earlier, and I've failed to make sales calls soon enough to retain a client, but not anymore. One thing I now absolutely ensure is that I take any action needed to nip things in the bud. I take the action needed daily, despite how I feel and despite any emotions I've attached to not taking the action.

You see, if you fail to take the action today, you will find you have even more reasons not to take the action tomorrow. You will have more reasons why you can't make the call, and you will have more reasons why you can't address whatever aspect of the business it is you're failing to tackle today. Of course, this extends beyond your business, it extends into all areas of life. Tomorrow will be a better day to start the diet, be healthier, remove stress, anger and frustration, and tomorrow will be a good day to kick that habit, but what about right now?

The mental and mindful choice to take action only takes a few seconds. The choice can be made right now to make those choices. The sooner you start to take action on the aspirations, dreams and desires that support the future version of self and your legacy, the sooner you begin to build momentum, and the more you take action in the present with your focus on the person you want to become as opposed to the person you once were, the more you can realise your goals, aspirations and dreams.

You can't just turn up and expect more.

You can't just turn up and expect more. You can't just turn up at work and expect things to happen; it takes continual positive action, continual effort, and continual growth and development. You see, the more you commit today to being more of the person you want to be, the more you will see the opportunities that support that person, and the more you will see opportunities to create greater earning potential, greater wealth, greater abundance and greater freedom.

Remember, if you need to find a few extra hours of free time this week to focus on expanding your business, what could you outsource or hand over to others to create that time? Now consider why you have not done this already? By letting go of the ego and the characters you have created, you begin to grow into a new version of you, a better version of you, and one that is constantly moving and striving towards what you want.

Now is the time to take action, but pause for today. Turn over the corner of the page, think about what needs to happen, the stakes you need to remove from yourself, and what actions you can take within the next twenty-four hours. What aspects of conversations do you need to change; what savings can be made; where are you spending money, and is this a wise investment? Are you reinvesting in the aspects of self that are going to produce the freedom you desire? Are you being truthful with self? If now is not the right time to take the action needed to make some fundamental changes, then when will be?

IF PEOPLE LIKE YOU, THEY'LL LISTEN TO YOU, BUT IF THEY TRUST YOU, THEY'LL DO BUSINESS WITH YOU.

CHAPTER FIVE – LOOKING FOR MENTORS

- Stop Second-Guessing What You're Worth
- Why You'll Need Help
- Delaying the Inevitable
- It Took Me Ten Years
- The Experts You'll Need – Look for The Best

Here we are in Chapter Five, a chapter in which I'm going to invite you to look for mentors. Mentors have always played a part in my life and certainly in my early career.

We've already discussed the value of networking and the benefits of relinquishing unsupportive people and influences, replacing them with people who are going to inspire and support you on your journey, but I now invite you to look for people and experts within your field who are really going to move you on and up to the next level; individuals who have the tools and skills to propel you to the next stage and move your business forward into bigger and greater things.

This is something that took me a while to get my head around in the earlier stages of my business. I didn't have the cash flow to invest in important mentors so I would try to second-guess everything I needed to know and then reverse engineer what I thought successful people in my field were doing. I was fearful of reaching out and asking for help, therefore I could always come up with all manner of reasons why a mentor would not be able to help me. But, all I was doing was delaying the inevitable.

Reach Out and Ask for Help

Now, there are many different people out there pretending they are experts. Business advisors that have never owned a business, and consultants that have never faced the challenges experienced by those they consult with, but there are also a lot of good quality informative mentors.

There are a people out there, including your competitors, who are willing to share their knowns, their knowledge and their understandings with you in exchange for some form of benefit or trade. In the early days, the restriction for me was tapping into this as I felt the need to protect what I had, shying away from sharing my secrets, my stories and my uniqueness, but, in truth, it doesn't matter how you try to protect any of that because it will come out anyway. It's for this reason that I invite you to avoid this action; avoid the temptation to believe someone is going to steal, copy or plagiarise your ideas. Avoid the temptation to delay the inevitable and reach out and ask for help instead.

If you have a specific weakness in terms of your business development and growth, or you lack understanding in any element of your industry, then reach out and find a mentor. Find someone to whom you'll be accountable week by week and minute by minute; someone who has experience in investment, experience in business growth and development, and has a proven track record.

There will come a time when you need help; there will come a time when you need mentors and investors if your business is to reach the next level, so why not start looking for those individuals right now. Identify the people who have the skills and the knowledge you need, the people who know how to take you to the next level. You may be trading locally but you want to trade internationally, so reach out and find mentors who have the understanding, knowledge and expertise you need because they can help you get to where you want to go in half or even quarter the amount of the time it might take you if you choose to figure it out on your own.

As food for thought, consider this...

Behind every successful person, there's a mentor who helped them to succeed.

- Oprah Winfrey was mentored by Maya Angelou, a celebrated author and poet. the late Maya Angelou.
- Mark Zuckerberg, Facebook CEO, was mentored by the late Steve Jobs, former Apple Inc. CEO.
- Mother Teresa devoted her life to helping others, but she also had a mentor: Father Michael van der Peet.
- And haute couture designer Yves St. Laurent was mentored by fashion designer Christian Dior.

We live in an age where reaching a global market is no more complicated than reaching a local market. Where you live is no longer a barrier to where you can trade. You can have your product or service appear on the front page of Google or any other search engine, you can pay to appear at the top of the list, and you can reach your target audience as they socialise through social media platforms. You can pop up in front of consumers of every age, race, faith, job title and background and from all over the world, so why not expand your vision. Why not start with the world as your market and then chunk backwards, finding the mentors and the people who can support you on that journey?

It requires the same amount of effort to market to an international audience as it does a local audience, but, of course, much depends on the service or product you offer. You may be offering a local service, but if you were to share the understanding and the knowledge with a global audience, how could this be re-packaged and sold to an international market? How can your skills be packaged, bottled and re-sold?

It took me ten years to find the right mentor.

It took me ten years to find the right mentor, so it took me ten years to stop restricting myself in a mindset of attempting to reverse engineer the knowledge and understanding of my competitors. The invitation here is to spend the next week searching for and looking out for the people that could help you to get to the next level. Avoid the temptation to make choices based on price alone, instead letting the deciding factor be value in terms of growth and development. Look locally and look globally, looking for mentors, perhaps competitors, who have experience in your specific market. Reach out and ask for help. You see, you may find that those who are ranked in a similar field to you are thinking the same.

Once you are at the top of the game, it's very hard to stay there, especially if those ranked second, third and fourth come together and share knowledge and understanding. I spent years being accountable to only myself, looking for advice and guidance but failing to accept it or act on it.

Look for the Best

If you need financial advice, seek the best financial advice. If you need legal advice, get the best legal advice you can. Best does not necessarily mean most expensive. If you have a budget, you can find some of the best professionals on outsourcing platforms at affordable prices, so reach out, see who's out there, and never fear asking for help.

Relinquish all limitations, realise your dream, and understand and accept that you can be more. And why wouldn't you be more? So, do it now; draft up a list of mentors you might need and the aspects of your business in which you have limited knowledge and knowns. Draft it, reach out, send the email, and book the appointment. The sooner you take action, the sooner you are giving yourself permission to grow your business into everything it deserves to be.

My final word of guidance on this is to look for those who are already achieving.

Look to those who have a proven track record, and look for evidence of their experience and understanding. Avoid the temptation to go with those who have the best-looking website or the glossiest magazines and materials, and look instead for positive feedback and testimonials. Set out clear and precise guidelines in terms of your expectations and your reasons for going to them, and choose your mentor based on the return and the value they bring to the business based on these expectations and reasons. The investment must be an investment. Ask for guarantees; remember these are your choices and you have the choice of signing up or looking elsewhere.

Look for those who are going to increase value and give you a return based on the terms of the contract you set out – cheapest is not always best, and most expensive is not necessarily best. If you need a bookkeeper, look for a bookkeeper who can give you exactly what you need and free up your time to grow and develop other aspects of your business. If you are looking for a marketing strategist, make sure they have a proven track record of success in this field; that they themselves are living testament to what they deliver.

For example, a marketing or social media marketing company with fifteen followers is clearly far behind a company with several hundreds of thousands of followers and suggests it may not be following its own advice or practising what it preaches.

Spend some time over the next few days thinking about who could benefit your business and identify the reasons why you might want to reach out to these individuals.

What would you be expecting from them? With this done, go ahead and send the email, make the call, and make the investment. But, make it an investment on your terms, not one based on their expectation of what they should deliver – why should it ever be any other way?

IF ONE
DOES NOT
KNOW TO
WHICH
PORT ONE
IS SAILING,
NO WIND IS
FAVORABLE.

DOESN'T YOUR BUSINESS DEPEND ON IT?

CHAPTER SIX – WHAT YOU ARE REALLY WORTH

- Time is Money – Shift in Thinking
- Practise What You Preach
- Best Use Of Time
- Minimise the Losses – See Big
- Live Off Less Than 10%
- Waste Less Invest More
- Show Don't Tell – Demonstration is Key
- How Much is Enough – More of What?

Welcome to Chapter Six. In this chapter, I'm going to talk about what you are really worth. We've already covered the details of what's going to be important to you, who you are, and the purpose and reasons behind setting up your business and why it's important to know this. Hopefully, you have completed the exercises and really chunked down to the specific emotions involved and questioned whether they're true or not. You've also questioned what money means to you, considered how much you're worth per minute, and identified where you've perhaps been wasting time in the past, dealing with tasks and aspects of your business that really would be better suited to someone else.

I am hopeful that all of this has unlocked a few previously unthought of or unanswered questions and that you're now starting to question whether you are doing things in the best way possible or following the right procedures. As I've said from the beginning, not everything detailed in this book is going to be of immediate relevance to you, I'm simply sharing my experiences and some of the things I've encountered along my journey as the owner of multiple businesses, some of which have done extremely well, some of which have struggled.

I'm sharing with you my knowledge and understanding, not any particular expertise, and I'm sure you will encounter many other people out there who are more than willing to share a different opinion of the right way to do things. This is purely my experience, and it's my hope that by sharing it with you, it may trigger additional thinking and thereby help you on your journey towards becoming who you want to be in the business you want to be in.

Time is Money

So, what are you really worth? In other words, if you were to put yourself out there and sell yourself, what value would you be happy and fulfilled with? If someone was to offer to hire you for a year and for 24 hours each day you'd belong to them, what value would you place on yourself? Now, I didn't mention money there for a reason, but I'm sure that a certain figure came to mind. So, with this being the case, time is money. I've said this already but I think it's very important to reinforce it here. Time is money. For me, every day has purpose and every minute has a value. If I'm not working, then I'm making sure that I'm investing every minute wisely. I've met so many people in my coaching practice who have invested years and years and years into the wrong journey. They've invested so much time, just not particularly wisely; they've invested their minutes in ways which they would change with the benefit of hindsight. Looking back, they realise that had they had more conscious control, more knowledge and more known, they would have changed what they're delivering.

So, time is money, and it's important to utilise this mindset within your business, irrespective of whether you run a billion-dollar company or you're just starting out with a turnover of less than a thousand dollars a month. Time is money, and it's the way you utilise and invest your time that determines how quickly you become successful.

Remove the restraints of what you believe to be true.

Remove the restraints of what you believe is true. Some people give you timelines. I've written and published a book within 24 hours before now, and I've recorded some of my most successful audios in a matter of hours, audios that have sold and helped millions of people around the world. Avoid slipping into the belief that a successful product or service takes months or even years to construct.

If the intention behind it is genuine and in alignment with the person you want to be and the foundations you have set in relation to your legacy, then there's no reason why you can't remove past restraints and move into a new mindset and a new space of providing or delivering within just a few hours.

Practise What You Preach

However, to move into this space, there's a key piece of information I need to share with you and that is to practise what you preach. You see, there are a lot of experts out there who do not, and the health and fitness industry provides some good examples. If a company is selling a "healthy" supplement that will provide X, Y and Z benefits to the consumer but they are not showcasing those benefits in themselves, then why would anyone buy into the product; if a nutritionist is promoting a weight loss diet that's guaranteed to help shed unwanted pounds and keep them off, yet they themselves are overweight, why on earth would anyone choose to follow any advice or guidance they provide?

If you are not practising what you preach, how can you expect your prospective clients or consumers to have faith in your knowledge, or have any confidence in your understanding of the product or service you're delivering?

Whether you are putting out a message as an expert or as someone with extensive knowledge in a particular field or service, you need to understand the importance of practising what you preach. Any promise you offer must be backed up with a guarantee to support it, and you must be living proof of the message you're conveying; you must demonstrate exactly what you mean, and to do so, your service or product must be in alignment with the person you want to be.

I've learned to go beyond practising what I preach and to live in the space of my clients and consumers. This has given me an understanding of their needs and wants, and thereby has minimised my losses. I've minimised the potential loss of good relationships through failing to deliver on a promise made, and I've maximised my understanding of the struggles faced by clients and potential clients.

When you immerse yourself in this space, you gain a true understanding of the expectations held and a true understanding of the needs and wants of the people paying for your products or services. There will be losses, people will venture off in other directions, but business is all about gaining new revenue while retaining as much as you can.

By practising what you preach and demonstrated the benefits of your product or service, through social media or otherwise, you gain trust and people buy into what you offer. This means that in times of reviewing where you're spending your money, or in times of cutbacks, you continue to offer value because your message is pure.

You'll continue to offer value because you'll understand that each product and service does have a shelf life and you'll know that after a certain amount of time there may be a need to create a bigger product for those who have exhausted the current range of products and services, and you can only really understand this through living in that space.

Living on Less Than 10%

Another important recommendation that must be mentioned here is to avoid having all of your eggs in one basket, in other words, avoid relying heavily on one source of income. This is a topic covered in greater detail in the following chapters but now is a good time to trigger further thinking. It's my belief that any business should function on less than 10% of the net turnover.

Now, I know there will be some mathematicians out there who will say that this is impossible, especially within the corporate world, but it's my belief that most of the successful businesses on the planet live within a figure of less than 10%. That's cost. If they were to lose 25% of their income overnight, or if they were to lose a contract that provided 30% of their annual turnover, they would still be strong enough to survive within that marketplace.

Avoid having all of your eggs in one basket.

To enter this space, you must be aware of the smaller costs and you must understand that there is no place for ego in your business. It means keeping your overheads and outgoings low, looking at the cost of employment versus the cost of outsourcing, and the value in your time versus the value of the time needed to complete a certain task or exercise. I've been in this place. I was running government funded training courses and had a call centre of staff. One day I received a call informing me that the government had cut all funding, months ahead of when we expected the funds to cease. Overnight, my workforce had nothing to do. I still had salaries to pay, venues to pay for, and lighting, heating and office space bills to pay, but I maximised my profit by reducing overheads or keeping them low, spreading our bets and becoming non-reliant on one specific source.

If you can adopt this mindset now and work towards living off less than 10%, then I can guarantee you one thing, your business will have a reinforced level of longevity. You will have what you need to have more and be more, and grow quicker and faster. You will be able to sleep better at night and when you reach the stage of employing staff, you will know that you will always be able to fulfil your responsibility to them and your business. The recommendation here is to waste less and invest more. The more time you spend investing in yourself and investing in your business growth and development rather than getting immersed in the drama of business, the quicker you'll redefine perhaps not only your industry, but also your niche within it.

Show, Don't Tell

Don't just tell, demonstrate. Demonstrate why you're the leader and demonstrate your understanding of all aspects of your business. Demonstrate why you are the market leader or a force to be reckoned with, and demonstrate your understanding of the needs and wants of your clients and consumers. Demonstrate further or extended delivery beyond the first purchase or first phase of your service; what's next? What can you offer them? Where is the upsell? Where do they go to? If you don't offer the answers or you don't have the solutions they're looking for, they'll look elsewhere for someone who does.

TASK:

How much is enough for you?

_____

_____

_____

_____

_____

What more do you need to be doing?

_____

_____

_____

_____

_____

What more should you be providing?

_____

_____

_____

_____

_____

_____

Where else do you want to go, and who do you want to be?

_____

_____

_____

_____

_____

_____

We are no longer living in a world where we can be reliant on one product or service. We can be good at producing one product or we can be good at providing one service, and we can have one key service, but wouldn't it be better to retain your clients for longer? Wouldn't it be better to retain their custom for longer by giving them the option to follow a path or journey with you? For example, if you have valued your time at X amount per minute, the high-ticket item in your business should be time with you. In my business, this equates to the high-ticket item being one-to-one coaching, with the other options of group mentoring, events and webinars, online training, books and audios and free material also on offer in a descending order of cost.

There is a journey, a path available to each of my clients. Perhaps they want to jump straight in to one-to-one coaching, bypassing other options, or perhaps they want to begin with a free product and then follow the path into a book or audio download, then perhaps an app or an online training programme... the options to continue and progress on a journey are there.

It's important to map out a journey, not only yours, but also your clients' as this is the way to ensure you are maximising the return on every consumer, effectively mapping out what each of our clients is worth to you over the lifetime of your business.

You see, I don't believe that every client is worth only the cheapest option, I believe they're worth the highest – it just takes some of them longer to get there than others. This is something only you can decide and it means understanding what each call and each minute of your time actually means in terms of long-term revenue. It's the decision you now need to make. Answer these questions honestly: How much is enough? And, what do your clients want more of and are you providing it for them?

JUST
BECAUSE
SOMETHING
DOESN'T DO
WHAT YOU
PLANNED
IT TO DO
DOESN'T
MEAN IT'S
USELESS.

DOESN'T YOUR BUSINESS DEPEND ON IT?

CHAPTER SEVEN – ESTABLISHING THE NEXT VENTURE

- Why Eggs Always Get Broken
- One Source is Riskier Than Spreading the Bets
- Get Out of the Comfort of Being One Character
- Organising Life and Business
- Avoiding Balance as the Focus

Here we are in Chapter Seven, a chapter in which I want to talk about the importance of always looking to establish new ventures. This is something I've already mentioned in this book and it's a topic I cover time and time again in much of the material I've produced over the years, so I consider it to be key.

You already know the value of looking to multiple revenues sources and looking beyond the skills, products or services you currently offer. I'd now like you to investigate this area further. For example, if you are distributing a product, perhaps consider enhancing your business by offering a consultancy service in which you guide and help others who want to get their products to market. This could be your high-ticket item. Or, on the flip side, if you are currently a consultancy business, how could you package and bundle the service you offer to provide an alternative for those who can't afford your fee? Is there an on-line programme, an audio series or a podcast? Is this something you could be producing and thereby reaching more people?

Some Eggs Will Get Broken

You see, some eggs will always get broken, and this reinforces the need to run your business on around 10% of the net turnover. If you lose a contract or you lose an important client, do you still have a sustainable business? If you are running on more than 10%, the answer may be no. I know too many people in the business world, and in the personal world, who push themselves to their financial max every single month.

They live beyond their means, and I don't see this as a habit that stops at any ocean, it's a global issue. People around the world have slipped into a mindset of debt being acceptable. It's considered okay to be in debt and we live in a culture where it's okay to finance sofas, kitchenware, appliances, vehicles... the list goes on. But, some eggs will always be broken. It doesn't matter how secure you feel, there is always a vulnerability in business.

It is absolutely key that you understand and acknowledge the very real possibility of losing a contract or losing an important client. Is your business sustainable? You must ensure that you are not living outside of your means or living outside the limits of what you can afford. Think about it now. Are you living outside the space in which you feel truly comfortable? If your income was halved overnight, would you be able to continue living the way you do? If the answer is no, then right now is the time to begin making some fundamental changes. Do you have a backup plan? This takes us neatly back to where we began – there is no security any more. Once upon a time, security was believed to be found in "a job for life".

Here in the United Kingdom, a secure career path may at one point have included working for the government, working as a civil servant or in the Post Office. Jobs for life may have included joining the police force, teaching, working on the railways, or in the banking industry, but in today's world of reforms, pensions cuts, and cut backs in general, **the only security is the security that you create**. It makes sense, doesn't it? If you think about it, having only one source of income is a much riskier strategy than spreading the bets.

I am not a gambling man, I work too hard for my money, but if I were, I certainly wouldn't be stacking all of my money on one number. I would be spreading my bets and playing multiple tables, ensuring that I'd have some means of backing-up my income by limiting the risk of potentially losing everything in one hit.

I know of one business that relied so heavily on one source of income that it did lose everything in one hit. The business depended on social media advertising and overnight the social media outlet changed its terms and conditions, meaning the company could no longer target the same specific demographic. The cost of advertising suddenly went through the roof. They had become so comfortable with one source of income, one way of generating leads and attracting new clients, that changes in the terms and conditions changed everything. Factors outside of their control meant they could no longer depend on their one source of income.

If you have an online product or service, avoid making the same mistake. Spread your bets and avoid the temptation to rely heavily on one source to generate leads. You can double down on sources that are currently generating leads and thereby providing an income and paying the bills, but make sure you do not neglect other sources that can be turned up should they also start to generate leads. It makes sense, one source is always going to be riskier than multiple sources.

Business is just an extension of life.

Let's move on to another equally important recommendation. Now is the time to get out of the zone of playing one (or many) characters in your business. The key message here is to understand the difference between character and personality. Your personality is the person you are when you are stripped bare; the person you are when there is nowhere to hide and there is no protection from anything, effectively the person you would be if you were alone on a desert island and removed from any need to act in any particular way. It's who you are.

Now, in business, there's a temptation to play many characters, but the more characters you play, the more likely it is that you'll become misaligned with your intention and purpose, and the more likely it is that you'll make mistakes. It's time to strip back the characters you are playing and to begin working in alignment with truth, **the true you**, and the person you want to become. The income of your business is just a by-product of living the life you want to live, and the more you start to realise the true potential of your business, the more important it is to understand that the business is just an extension of life.

Avoid "Balance"

There is no work life balance. In fact, even the term "work life balance" is something I can't stand. It seems to have become a cultural fixation, something we're told we should be striving for, but there is no work life balance. There is life, there is living, there is being, but avoid the temptation to believe there is a work life balance to be had, because there isn't.

Avoid the temptation to invest heavily in a business, a path, or a journey that provides misery, unhappiness, hatred, anger, frustration and envy. If you are currently employed and looking to set up on your own or begin working for yourself, you have perhaps realised that there is no such thing as job security and you believe that now is the right time to take the jump.

However, ensure that whatever you do, whatever options you take, and whatever choices you make, your intention is to enhance life, promote better living and a better life. You must be able to wake up every morning feeling passionate about what you do and excited about your day ahead. If you're looking for balance, does this mean that you're only tolerating the work aspect to get to the life aspect? So many people in the world are unhappy because they are looking for balance, but what does that even mean? Does it mean that you're enduring time in an environment that isn't suitable for you? Are you valuing your personal time more than your business time?

If so, how are you able to commit fully and give your business exactly what it needs? Now is the time to realise that there is no work life balance, there is only life. Now is the time to make the choice to be more of the person you want to be and to up your game, taking your business and your life to the next level. Remember, you are the author of your own destiny. You are the author of your life. You have control. You have control over the choices you make; you have control over where you invest your time, and you have control over who you are to become.

The invitation right here and now is to stop wasting life. Stop wasting time living someone else's dream. Stop wasting the opportunities that are given to you daily, and remove yourself from the fear state of believing that everything is going to be okay, because it won't. Some of your eggs will be broken.

So, where are you investing your time right now? What are you doing to ensure that you spread the bet?

_____

_____

_____

_____

_____

_____

What characters need to be removed and who is the true personality behind your business?

_____

_____

_____

_____

What does that person want, and isn't it time to start realising that dream?

_____

_____

_____

_____

_____

_____

IF YOU HAVE ONE GOOD IDEA, PEOPLE WILL LEND YOU TWENTY.

DOESN'T YOUR BUSINESS DEPEND ON IT?

CHAPTER EIGHT – DUPLICATION IS THE ANSWER

- Once it Works, Duplicate
- Alternative Markets with the Same Product
- Multiple Incomes from One Venture
- Being Rich and Living Poor

Welcome to Chapter Eight. By now, I am hopeful that you have established the importance of building great foundations in your business and in all aspects of life. Perhaps you have come to the realisation that your business isn't as secure as you thought it was, and in this chapter I want to explore some of the factors and aspects of business and life that I have found to be of use.

Avoid Sitting Still

Again, it may not be relevant to your business right now or it may not be the best time to explore this, but I want to throw the topic of duplication out there for you to consider because if something is working, in business or in life, duplicating it is the best way to maximise its potential. In business, once you have a strategy in place that's making money and making your business more successful, duplicate it. It's important to avoid complacency in business. If you have a system that's working, you need to maximise its potential by duplicating it so that your whole business benefits, and this means avoiding the temptation to sit still.

I invite you now to work on a strategy to get you from a standstill to earning money. This may or may not be a passive income, but this is irrelevant and it matters only that you have something that's working and something you can duplicate. I have been doing this for years, re-branding and re-utilising the same product to maximise its earning potential.

The invitation here is to look at what you are currently doing, what is working, and how you might duplicate this in the coming weeks. You are not going to have to go through the whole learning process again, there is no need, and you may or may not be targeting a different demographic within the same industry. Either way, you already know what needs to be done, you've already gone through it and the challenges it created, so now is the time to maximise the time already invested by duplicating the process.

Duplication is the answer.

Many business owners fail to take action on this. They rely on the one product or service that's working and fail to look for ways to duplicate it. They believe they are only good for one thing, good for one market, and while it may be true that they have expertise in a particular market or they are specialists in a particular field, there is no reason why the product or service they offer cannot be duplicated and presented in another market. It can be done as a side-line, there's no need to drop everything to focus on it. It can be run in the background, requiring no more than an hour a day or even ten minutes when there's something that needs to be done.

It can be outsourced, or the price can be increased, but it's something that can be duplicated. I have known business owners who dominate a specific market and a localised market, yet they fail to duplicate what they have and effectively forget about targeting the rest of the world. In my one-to-one coaching business, 90% of my revenue is generated overseas but I am still able to deliver a professional and highly responsive service.

Mobile communication makes it possible to operate from any location in the world at any time. I've been in the jungle in Costa Rica and still managed to deliver a high level of service, so you see, the only excuses you have are the ones you choose to create.

You may be living in a small village with a limited population, but why not take your business online and expand beyond your local area? Why not target areas of greater wealth and areas where your knowledge and expertise is in demand? There is no reason why getting an understand of a different demographic or market should be limited to staying local. Unless you choose to stay local, you may well find that the online aspect of your business takes over and reaching out to a different demographic in different parts of the world becomes the focus of your business and the main money earner.

When I say that the world is an open opportunity, these are not just empty words. There are many ways to venture out from just one product and one market. Increase your personal value, your value per minute, and with this increase you bring greater value in terms of what you offer and you break through the barriers of what people are willing to pay. Why limit yourself?

Re-engineer what you offer and target a new audience, a global audience, and look at ways to maximise the time and effort you have already invested in your business. You see, it's all relevant. A billionaire will think nothing of investing $100,000 on hiring the services of a legal consultant for a day. An individual earning $100,000 per year may or may not hesitate over investing $5000 in the services of a leading consultant for a day, and while a business charging $50 per hour for their services may not be targeting the same audience as a business charging $500 per hour for their services, they both have access to the same global audience.

The only restrictions we have are the restrictions we place on ourselves.

The only restrictions we have are the restrictions we place on ourselves. The sooner you start living in a rich mindset, and by rich, I mean in terms of fulfilment rather than financially, the sooner those self-imposed restrictions can be overcome. In a rich mindset, rich in health, fitness, mindfulness and fulfilment, you begin to alter your beliefs over what it's possible for you to achieve. The alterations that allow you to duplicate are not system alterations but mindset alterations, and by shifting your mindset, you shift away from seeing restrictions to seeing opportunities. Could you double your price today? Would your audience still pay the price? If you have something that's working, why not duplicate it? If one person has found value in the product or service you offer, then there will be another willing to pay for it. Start being rich and avoid living in a poor mindset. Offer your product or services to the masses and adopt a mindset of being deserving.

Be Rich

Right now, you have a choice. Do you want to stay where you are, restricted to one or two products or services, or do you want to duplicate and maximise the earning potential of those products or services? Of course, this strategy is not necessarily going to be applicable to everyone in their business right now, but if you are reading this book, you have what you need to utilise all the knowledge in the world. If you can read, you have all you need to immerse yourself in the learnings of others, the strategies of others, and you have the option to then duplicate their skills and their understanding in processes and strategies. When something is working, all you need to do is understand the nuts and bolts of why it is working and then you have an opportunity to do the same.

You have what you need to be more of the person you want to be, so the invitation here is to be rich and avoid the temptation to live in a poor mindset. I believe in you, and I believe that you have it in you to become the person you want to be simply by making a few alterations and a few small shifts in your thought processes.

GREAT COMPANIES ARE BUILT ON GREAT PRODUCTS.

DOESN'T YOUR BUSINESS DEPEND ON IT?

CHAPTER NINE – INNER PRODUCTIVITY AND PURPOSE

- Deciding What You Really Want
- Knowing What You Want
- Moving On Those Actions
- Letting Go of the Drama
- Dealing with Anger, Resentment, Fear and Frustration

In this chapter, we are going to talk about productivity and purpose. This is something that was raised in Chapter One where we discussed the importance of finding out what it is you really want and then understanding that what you want has little to do with the tangible assets or tangible items in your life, but more the attachments and emotional connections you have with them.

Know What You Want

You see, if it's an Aston Martin you want, the very latest model with all the associated trappings, then it's going to cost you $250,000, but it's not actually the car or any of the all-singing-all-dancing trappings you want, it's the feelings, emotions and connections you have attached to owning such a car.

These attachments can be good or bad, but all we need to do here is look at legacy. Legacy is something I talk about a lot in my work but it's important for you to understand that legacy is more than just a word that's banded about in relation to the way people are going to remember you in years to come.

Legacy is about what you are going to give. I'm a follower of inspirational business people such as Sir Richard Branson and the late Dame Anita Roddick, founder of The Body Shop. Anita's story of creating an ethical brand has reached into every corner of the planet, and she was brought up in a fish and chip shop not far from where I live now. She has left a legacy. She is helping people to grow and develop, she is feeding people, and she is housing people years beyond her death. Now, this may not be the intention you have in setting up your business but I want you to really understand what your purpose is, and the reasons why you are doing what you doing – and you can do this by legacy.

What I am going to ask you to do is to imagine ten lifetimes from now, the time of your children's children's children's children... you get the idea. Now think about what you could be doing right now to leave a legacy, something your descendants will still be talking about in ten lifetimes from now.

TASK:

What are you doing minute by minute, hour by hour, day by day, week by week, month by month and year by year that is contributing towards and supporting that legacy?

_____

_____

_____

_____

_____

_____

_____

_____

It's not everyone's intention to leave something behind; a trust, an estate, or an income for generations to come, and it needn't be related to money at all. It may be an ethic or a message, anything at all, but thinking about it now provides an opportunity to assess whether your daily actions are keeping you aligned to this legacy.

Your Legacy Statement

It's my belief that as we awaken every day, not only are we motivated by certain things, we also target certain things. We're heading towards a target, a destination, and our mind is controlling each of the choices we make. However, there are times when our target destination may have been created by another and not consciously created by ourselves, and it's by consciously creating a legacy for ourselves that we can begin to question our inherited beliefs and realign ourselves with the way we want to be remembered.

Through creating a legacy statement, we can question the things we have been told we should be doing, the rules we should be abiding by, and every other restriction of social conformity. We often live in this space through fear of judgement if we step away from it, but it's generally the case that those who can live outside of it are the most successful in life because they see opportunities that are missed by those trapped inside.

So, the invitation here is to create a statement of no more than 250 words; a statement that outlines how you want to be remembered, what your legacy might look like, who it might appeal to, and what it might look like for you.

TASK:

My legacy statement…

_____

Now, as you are working on this legacy, consider if you are making choices and taking actions in every moment based on the person you want to become, or if you are basing your choices and actions on becoming the person you have been told you shouldn't be. Are you motivating and inspiring yourself with an image you have created of the future, or are you being pushed along through fear of something, fear of loss? Are you running away or are you running towards? There is a big difference in the emotional connection.

Remove the Drama

The imitation right here and now in this very moment is to create a legacy, and then move on to take those actions and make the choice to be more of the person you want to be as opposed to being less of the person you don't want to be. With this said, there are going to be some key elements here and it's important to drive home the earlier message that you need to let go of the drama in your life.

If you have been living around people who no longer support the person you want to be, or living around people who only talk about the dramas and the negativity of the world, then understand that it's not possible to consciously protect yourself from them. The brain can only process so many basic items of information per second. Everything is filtered based on past learnings, knowledge and knows, and this enables you to think based on those understandings. Without those filters, you would overload the mind, you would vegetate.

So, the more conscious effort you give to removing the drama, the more you give yourself the breathing space you need to absorb the positivity in life. If you were to go to your social media page and remove all the people who talk about dramas and issues (I'm pretty sure you've got a few of those) and then only follow and subscribe to those who add benefit and value to the person you want to become, how quickly do you think you would start to think in a more productive state?

Of course, this is not only relevant to business. If you begin to shift and move into a space where you are surrounded by people who are supportive of your goals and aspirations, you may find that more people want to help. It's my belief that the more you reach out and ask for help, the more help is available to you.

We have no control over the past.

People are fearful of judgment, they're fearful of asking for help, but I believe that people want to share their story, they want to help people grow and develop, and deep down we are all good people. Everyone has good in them, we've just been blinkered by events in the outside world and it has become hard for us to filter through all the mess, the drama, the anger, fear, frustration and resentment of it all to see it.

By creating a legacy statement for you, you realign yourself with who and what you want to become as opposed to who you once were. We have no control over the past, it's gone and the opportunity to change it has gone, that's why we call it the past. The only true opportunity and choice you have is in the present moment, so wouldn't it make more sense to focus the choices you make and actions you take on becoming the person you want to be as opposed to not being the person you once were?

Create your legacy, write it out down, and then give yourself 24 hours to digest it. Think about the alterations you would like to make, and be selfish with this. This is *your* legacy and not that of a loved one, so be completely selfish and think about what you want and why it makes sense to *you*. The choice is yours to make, I don't have all the answers and I certainly can't provide every answer in this book, but, one thing I can guarantee and can be sure of is that the more you work in alignment with the person you want to be, the more committed you will be to your business venture, the more committed you will be to the actions you take, and the more you will remove the aspects of life that are no longer important – the drama and the distractions of the outside world.

Remove the Distractions

It's easy for us to get distracted in any given moment when we don't have a destination. You wouldn't just jump in your car and to start to drive without a destination; you wouldn't know what road to take or which signs to follow if you didn't have a destination, and you have the same lack of direction if you have no planned destination for your business.

Perhaps you have a golden intention for your business but it's not in alignment with the person you want to be, and you're struggling to find happiness and fulfilment in the illusive work life balance you've been conditioned to believe you should have. Remember, it doesn't exist.

You need to find happiness and fulfilment in life. Break down the divide between business and life and just have life. If it's your aspiration in business to be able to spend more time with your family, then why not just spend more time with your family. If your income is preventing you from doing so, then look carefully at where you have been investing your money; could you have one day off each week and choose a car that doesn't require such a huge investment every month?

Would this not give you the freedom to do exactly what you want if it's your goal is to spend more time with your family? To have what you want, you need to reduce the number of hours you work each week, and this means removing the distractions that are preventing you from maximising your minutes.

You see, we get caught up in valuing the wrong things; we get caught up in creating false values, and creating perceptions of what we cannot have as opposed to what we can, creating reasons because we're fearful of the possibility that we can have exactly what we want. So, the invitation now is to pause for the next 24 hours, avoid the temptation to read on or to make any changes, think about your legacy statement, who you want to become, and perhaps the reasons why you have not been fulfilling this up until this point.

Think also about why you have perhaps been sabotaging the fulfilment of your goals, dreams and aspirations. Is it because once you fulfil these, you may become lost? By setting a legacy, you set something so far into the distance that it is unachievable in your lifetime, yet you wake up every day feeling motivated and inspired by that vision of the future. Think about what you want, and what you want to give that will be remembered in ten generations from now, and I'm certain that you will start to make some changes almost immediately; you will start living and being more of the person you want to be.

MY SUCCESS JUST EVOLVED FROM WORKING HARD AT THE BUSINESS AT HAND EACH DAY.

DOESN'T YOUR BUSINESS DEPEND ON IT?

CHAPTER TEN – WHAT NEXT?

- Letting Go of Your Vulnerability
- Breaking Through the Perception
- Knowing That You Are the Truth
- Everything Else Isn't Real
- Why NOW is the Time

Welcome to Chapter Ten. In this final chapter, I want to talk about the need to let go of vulnerability. By this, I mean the need to remove yourself from the judgement of others and the person others perceive you to be so that you can become who you really want to be.

I'm going to invite you to think for a moment about all the things you need to let go of to become more of the business owner, more of the entrepreneur, and more of the person you want to be.

TASK:

What happens if you begin allowing yourself to be the person you want to be?

_____

_____

_____

_____

_____

_____

_____

_____

What happens if start to realise your dreams and begin removing elements of your life that you've only kept through being fearful of how others might feel?

_____

_____

_____

_____

_____

_____

_____

_____

_____

I believe that everyone can be more of the person they want to be. What happens when you start to own it? What happens when you put yourself, the person you want to be, first and stop concerning yourself with others? To have and be greater things, especially in terms of business, you need to release all limiting emotional attachments to the past and any limiting inherited beliefs. You become vulnerable, but understand that your vulnerability is in fact your strength, and the stronger you are the more vulnerable you can be. Vulnerability should not be feared, it demonstrates that you have a greater understanding of yourself and a more advanced level of self-awareness than others, so now is the time to let go of any attachments you have in relation to being vulnerable.

Be Vulnerable

Be vulnerable, embrace vulnerability. Embrace criticism and embrace feedback, because, as you already know, those who project it may only be doing so through their own lack of fulfilment, not because it's truth. You have the choice to either accept their version of reality or not, and the choice to be inspired by the actions of others or not. Sadly, there are people out there who are not going to be inspired by your success, your forward movement, your dreams and aspirations because it reflects badly on them.

Vulnerability only comes with viability. The ability to do something.

For me, vulnerability means movement, action, and the ability to do something about it. To break through into this new space, create a new perception of what's possible. Author your own destiny. Author your own day, your own diary. Start today with a blank page in your diary and outline all the things you want for today, the things you want to accomplish.

The athlete's journal (available on Amazon) works by spring-boarding the user from one day to the next. Every day is set to inspire you to move forward to the next, to jump through the hoops of today so that you have the freedom to do more of what you want tomorrow. This is because the only truth is your truth, and the only truth there is, is the truth you create.

Understand this and accept this – the only reality is your reality. It's key to understand and accept that the beliefs of another are only a figment of their mind, their beliefs, their world, and their visions. Anything is possible when you put your mind to it. It doesn't have to deliver in terms of being a tangible item, but the connection is so much greater when you believe in something and connect with it on an emotional or spiritual level that can't be quantified.

The truth is that you create your own truth and nothing else is real.

The truth is that you create your own truth and nothing else is real. The reason I've written this book is not to give you guidance on how to market in the best way possible, or how to increase your profits over the next six months, or how to be the next billionaire, but to create an internal understanding of what is required of you to be the business owner you want to be and one you can be proud of; the entrepreneur who goes on to achieve more, and to overcome the internal objections rather than those of external influences out with your control.

The only thing you have control over is the present; the only thing you have control over are the choices you make in the present moment. Everything else is a figment of your imagination. It hasn't happened. The memories of the past are simply that, memories. The thing you think you can remember from ten years ago is not what you're remembering, you're only remembering the last memory.

If you thought about it twenty minutes ago, your thoughts will only go to that thought of twenty minutes ago, they're not going to the memory of the past. And, because so much has happened and so many learnings have taken place, that memory has just become a figment of your imagination. It's not the truth, it's fragmented, based on so many other things and the filters you've created.

Why Wouldn't You Have the Life You Want?

The choice right now is either to reflect on the past, and the things you've not done or not achieved; reflect on the past and create more of what the past offered, or look to the future and understand that in taking action to be more of the person you want to be and have more of the things you want to have will guide the decisions and choices you make in a completely different way. You enter a new realm of choice making – and why wouldn't you? Why would you not have the life you want? Why would you not utilise business in the way in which it's intended, and that's to add value to your life? What have you been waiting for?

TASK:

What else do you need to clear out from the past?

_____

_____

_____

_____

_____

What do you need to let go of?

_____

_____

_____

_____

_____

And why is now the right time to become more of the person you want to be?

_____

_____

_____

_____

_____

If you're ready now to make the jump and to do exactly what you want in life and in business, then I'm going to ask you to do one thing: **be truthful with yourself**. Be truthful and act in alignment with that truth. Be truthful in the present, always, and ensure that the choices you make are always entertaining that truth. That version of truth may change as you evolve within your business, and this is fine, but the key focus must always be to remain truthful to self.

THE CHOICE IS ONLY YOURS TO MAKE.

HELP!!!

I need to ask you a favour.

If you got anything out of this book, if you highlighted something that made an impact on the way you think, or perhaps improved the quality of your thinking, then I hope you'll do something for me – pass it on.

If you've scribbled in it and want to keep it then I understand; if you've scribbled in it and you're willing to share those notes with a stranger, then drop it off at your local coffee shop or leave it somewhere....

I need this support. I want to help action takers just like you to make the shifts required to be great.

Spread the word, perhaps share an image of your favourite paragraph or leave a review on Amazon.

Thanks, Benjamin

WHAT IS NEXT FOR YOU?

A QUICK LESSON ON BREATH

Before starting work with a client, not only do I review the notes and bring myself into the present, I also spend a moment bringing conscious thought to my breath. This is an exercise I also recommend to each one of my clients.

Taking a moment to bring conscious thought to your breath acts like a transitioning mechanism *releasing you* from past moments and moving you into the next. (Think momentarily about just one event where a transitioning mechanism may help you.)

Moving on.

If you have been following me for any length of time, you will know that I've produced some of the world's leading meditation audiobooks, one of which, And Breathe Now, regularly leading the charts with over 250 000 downloads. With numbers increasing daily, the benefits are reaching every corner of the globe.

Centring the breath has met with some resistance over the last 20 or 30 years, but it's a technique that's becoming

more acceptable in modern-day life. However, despite
the *increasing acceptance*, I'm surprised to find there's still
resistance among those seeking to increase their level of
performance.

To me, all starts with the breath: from the way we're able to
communicate verbally to the oxygenation of the blood, the
breath has the ability to choke us, or fill us with confidence.

If you can master control over your breath, you are already
several steps ahead of where you think you should be. To
those who haven't yet mastered breath, I invite you to follow
through with the following exercise. However, this should
be done with no expectation of what you might experience;
just *enjoy the present* moment, commit to the act of just
doing, and notice the element of control it brings.

First things first, go through the experience and try it
for yourself. Many people report that once they've gone
through the process a couple of times they feel best
when they close their eyes and *relax* in a seated or laying
position.

Exercise:

Start by taking five deep breaths… bring your awareness
to the rise and fall of the chest… as you breathe out, notice
muscles around the shoulders and neck relaxing very
slightly… the muscles perhaps around the face relaxing…
the opening of the mouth… the breath deepening… taking
two further deep breaths… allowing any thoughts on
the mind to drift away completely… as breath alone now
relaxes you further… noticing all of the large muscle groups

relaxing… perhaps becoming heavier with every outward breath… noticing a rhythm appearing between relaxation and the rise and fall of your chest… now… just enjoying this… for a few moments…

Any warmth within the body just releasing now… perhaps any pain or tension… relaxing and releasing with every breath… drifting away to a place where you can allow any thoughts to disappear and you reach a place of no-mind… perhaps expanding any remaining thoughts to the edges of your current environment… the rooms… building, or county… over the seas, or perhaps into the sky… every breath releasing and relaxing you that bit further…

End.

You can practise this at any stage – pre, during or post-event – and the more you commit to evolving and developing to suit your specific requirements, the more you will benefit from the results it brings.

This, of course, is simply a guideline, but it's a quick and easy exercise that will help you to find centred breath.

4 WEEK DIARY

AM I DESERVING RIGHT NOW...

My desired results for today are:

Positive declarations and/or actions for generating and creating forward momentum.

Fitness focus

I want to complete today:

Nutrition focus

What I am prepared to do to achieve this?

Mindset focus

What improvements can I make based on yesterday?

Thoughts and ideas:

Positive intentions of the day:

WHAT CAN I DO RIGHT NOW...

My desired results for today are:

Positive declarations and/or actions for generating and creating forward momentum.

Fitness focus

I want to complete today:

Nutrition focus

What I am prepared to do to achieve this?

Mindset focus

What improvements can I make based on yesterday?

Thoughts and ideas:

Positive intentions of the day:

BEING 10% BETTER RIGHT NOW...

My desired results for today are:

Positive declarations and/or actions for generating and creating forward momentum.

Fitness focus

I want to complete today:

Nutrition focus

What I am prepared to do to achieve this?

Mindset focus

What improvements can I make based on yesterday?

Thoughts and ideas:

Positive intentions of the day.

WHAT IS
REQUIRED NOW...

My desired results for today are:

Positive declarations and/or actions for generating and creating forward momentum.

Fitness focus

I want to complete today:

Nutrition focus

What I am prepared to do to achieve this?

Mindset focus

What improvements can I make based on yesterday?

Thoughts and ideas:

Positive intentions of the day:

ARE YOU BEING TRUE RIGHT NOW...

My desired results for today are:

Positive declarations and/or actions for generating and creating forward momentum.

Fitness focus

I want to complete today:

Nutrition focus

What I am prepared to do to achieve this?

Mindset focus

What improvements can I make based on yesterday?

Thoughts and ideas:

Positive intentions of the day:

WHAT IT TAKES RIGHT NOW...

My desired results for today are:

Positive declarations and/or actions for generating and creating forward momentum.

Fitness focus

I want to complete today:

Nutrition focus

What I am prepared to do to achieve this?

Mindset focus

What improvements can I make based on yesterday?

Thoughts and ideas:

Positive intentions of the day:

IN THE PRESENT RIGHT NOW...

My desired results for today are:

Positive declarations and/or actions for generating and creating forward momentum.

Fitness focus

I want to complete today:

Nutrition focus

What I am prepared to do to achieve this?

Mindset focus

What improvements can I make based on yesterday?

Thoughts and ideas:

Positive intentions of the day:

AM I DESERVING RIGHT NOW...

My desired results for today are:

Positive declarations and/or actions for generating and creating forward momentum.

Fitness focus

I want to complete today:

Nutrition focus

What I am prepared to do to achieve this?

Mindset focus

What improvements can I make based on yesterday?

Thoughts and ideas:

Positive intentions of the day:

WHAT CAN I DO RIGHT NOW...

My desired results for today are:

Positive declarations and/or actions for generating and creating forward momentum.

Fitness focus

I want to complete today:

Nutrition focus

What I am prepared to do to achieve this?

Mindset focus

What improvements can I make based on yesterday?

Thoughts and ideas:

Positive intentions of the day:

BEING 10% BETTER RIGHT NOW...

My desired results for today are:

Positive declarations and/or actions for generating and creating forward momentum.

Fitness focus

I want to complete today:

Nutrition focus

What I am prepared to do to achieve this?

Mindset focus

What improvements can I make based on yesterday?

Thoughts and ideas:

Positive intentions of the day:

WHAT IS REQUIRED NOW...

My desired results for today are:

Positive declarations and/or actions for generating and creating forward momentum.

Fitness focus

I want to complete today:

Nutrition focus

What I am prepared to do to achieve this?

Mindset focus

What improvements can I make based on yesterday?

Thoughts and ideas:

Positive intentions of the day:

ARE YOU BEING TRUE RIGHT NOW...

My desired results for today are:

Positive declarations and/or actions for generating and creating forward momentum.

Fitness focus

I want to complete today:

Nutrition focus

What I am prepared to do to achieve this?

Mindset focus

What improvements can I make based on yesterday?

Thoughts and ideas:

Positive intentions of the day:

WHAT IT TAKES RIGHT NOW...

My desired results for today are:

Positive declarations and/or actions for generating and creating forward momentum.

Fitness focus

I want to complete today:

Nutrition focus

What I am prepared to do to achieve this?

Mindset focus

What improvements can I make based on yesterday?

Thoughts and ideas:

Positive intentions of the day:

IN THE PRESENT RIGHT NOW...

My desired results for today are:

Positive declarations and/or actions for generating and creating forward momentum.

Fitness focus

I want to complete today:

Nutrition focus

What I am prepared to do to achieve this?

Mindset focus

What improvements can I make based on yesterday?

Thoughts and ideas:

Positive intentions of the day:

AM I DESERVING RIGHT NOW...

My desired results for today are:

Positive declarations and/or actions for generating and creating forward momentum.

Fitness focus

I want to complete today:

Nutrition focus

What I am prepared to do to achieve this?

Mindset focus

What improvements can I make based on yesterday?

Thoughts and ideas:

Positive intentions of the day.

WHAT CAN I DO RIGHT NOW...

My desired results for today are:

Positive declarations and/or actions for generating and creating forward momentum.

Fitness focus

I want to complete today:

Nutrition focus

What I am prepared to do to achieve this?

Mindset focus

What improvements can I make based on yesterday?

Thoughts and ideas:

Positive intentions of the day:

BEING 10% BETTER RIGHT NOW...

My desired results for today are:

Positive declarations and/or actions for generating and creating forward momentum.

Fitness focus

I want to complete today:

Nutrition focus

What I am prepared to do to achieve this?

Mindset focus

What improvements can I make based on yesterday?

Thoughts and ideas:

Positive intentions of the day:

WHAT IS REQUIRED NOW...

My desired results for today are:

Positive declarations and/or actions for generating and creating forward momentum.

Fitness focus

I want to complete today:

Nutrition focus

What I am prepared to do to achieve this?

Mindset focus

What improvements can I make based on yesterday?

Thoughts and ideas:

Positive intentions of the day:

ARE YOU BEING TRUE RIGHT NOW...

My desired results for today are:

Positive declarations and/or actions for generating and creating forward momentum.

Fitness focus

I want to complete today:

Nutrition focus

What I am prepared to do to achieve this?

Mindset focus

What improvements can I make based on yesterday?

Thoughts and ideas:

Positive intentions of the day:

WHAT IT TAKES RIGHT NOW...

My desired results for today are:

Positive declarations and/or actions for generating and creating forward momentum.

Fitness focus

I want to complete today:

Nutrition focus

What I am prepared to do to achieve this?

Mindset focus

What improvements can I make based on yesterday?

Thoughts and ideas:

Positive intentions of the day:

IN THE PRESENT RIGHT NOW...

My desired results for today are:

Positive declarations and/or actions for generating and creating forward momentum.

Fitness focus

I want to complete today:

Nutrition focus

What I am prepared to do to achieve this?

Mindset focus

What improvements can I make based on yesterday?

Thoughts and ideas:

Positive intentions of the day:

AM I DESERVING RIGHT NOW...

My desired results for today are:

Positive declarations and/or actions for generating and creating forward momentum.

Fitness focus

I want to complete today:

Nutrition focus

What I am prepared to do to achieve this?

Mindset focus

What improvements can I make based on yesterday?

Thoughts and ideas:

Positive intentions of the day:

WHAT CAN I DO RIGHT NOW...

My desired results for today are:

Positive declarations and/or actions for generating and creating forward momentum.

Fitness focus

I want to complete today:

Nutrition focus

What I am prepared to do to achieve this?

Mindset focus

What improvements can I make based on yesterday?

Thoughts and ideas:

Positive intentions of the day:

BEING 10% BETTER RIGHT NOW...

My desired results for today are:

Positive declarations and/or actions for generating and creating forward momentum.

Fitness focus

I want to complete today:

Nutrition focus

What I am prepared to do to achieve this?

Mindset focus

What improvements can I make based on yesterday?

Thoughts and ideas:

Positive intentions of the day:

WHAT IS REQUIRED NOW...

My desired results for today are:

Positive declarations and/or actions for generating and creating forward momentum.

Fitness focus

I want to complete today:

Nutrition focus

What I am prepared to do to achieve this?

Mindset focus

What improvements can I make based on yesterday?

Thoughts and ideas:

Positive intentions of the day:

ARE YOU BEING TRUE RIGHT NOW...

My desired results for today are:

Positive declarations and/or actions for generating and creating forward momentum.

Fitness focus

I want to complete today:

Nutrition focus

What I am prepared to do to achieve this?

Mindset focus

What improvements can I make based on yesterday?

Thoughts and ideas:

Positive intentions of the day.

WHAT IT TAKES RIGHT NOW...

My desired results for today are:

Positive declarations and/or actions for generating and creating forward momentum.

Fitness focus

I want to complete today:

Nutrition focus

What I am prepared to do to achieve this?

Mindset focus

What improvements can I make based on yesterday?

Thoughts and ideas:

Positive intentions of the day:

IN THE PRESENT RIGHT NOW...

My desired results for today are:

Positive declarations and/or actions for generating and creating forward momentum.

Fitness focus

I want to complete today:

Nutrition focus

What I am prepared to do to achieve this?

Mindset focus

What improvements can I make based on yesterday?

Thoughts and ideas:

Positive intentions of the day:

www.ingramcontent.com/pod-product-compliance
Lightning Source LLC
Chambersburg PA
CBHW051803170526
45167CB00005B/1859